Overcoming Frustration and Anger

Overcoming Frustration and Anger

by PAUL A. HAUCK

THE WESTMINSTER PRESS
PHILADELPHIA

PUBLISHED BY THE WESTMINSTER PRESS

®

PHILADELPHIA, PENNSYLVANIA

PRINTED IN THE UNITED STATES OF AMERICA

10   11   12   13   14   15

Library of Congress Cataloging in Publication Data

Hauck, Paul A.
  Overcoming frustration and anger.

  1. Anger. 2. Frustration. 3. Rational-
emotive psychotherapy. I. Title.
[DNLM: 1. Anger—Popular works. 2. Frustration—
Popular works. 3. Mental health—Popular works.
BF575.A5 H368o 1974 / WM75 H368o 1974]
BF575.A5H35   131'.33   73-20285
ISBN 0-664-24983-3

To Marcie

Contents

Preface

ANGER IS NOT ONLY A VERY UNCOMFORTABLE EMOTIONAL state, it is also a potentially very dangerous one. All of us know what this means, because one or more times during our lives we have all been pushed to a point where we could have become violent or in many cases actually did become so. Jails are filled with violent men, marriages are broken because hatred developed between two people who once loved each other dearly, and the crime rate in society has risen because millions of us have responded to frustrations with increased bitterness and anger.

It is time that we understood this emotion. It is time that we consider other ways of responding to frustrations. It is not necessary that we become bitter, spiteful, or resentful simply because we are not getting our way. Unfortunately, understanding the psychology of anger has been lacking to the general public, and it is for this reason that I undertook the writing of this book. Becoming an unangry person is not so difficult if one is first shown how to achieve an unangry state. The discussions of case material and of techniques that follow in these pages will give a reader all that he needs to know to master his self-righteous indignation. You can, if you apply yourself vigorously enough, learn to overcome anger for the rest of your life for all practical purposes. You will also learn how to be a firm and self-assertive person who does not let others walk over him, but who manages to do this in a civil and polite way. If this has been your desire and you have found it impossible to achieve, then read on and apply the principles you are about to discover.

P.A.H.

1

After Thirty Years
of Fighting, A Smile

IT WAS DURING THE THIRD SESSION WITH MS. BAKER that she finally took my advice seriously and decided I might have something worthwhile to offer her though it sounded crazy.

"I can appreciate the fact," I summarized, "that living with a drinking husband for thirty years is no picnic. The fact that he is spending the family fortune for drinking is also very tough to take. But the fact that he curses you up one side and down the other every Tuesday, Thursday, and Saturday does not mean you have to get angry with the old boy. He's just being a poor sick fellow who can't help himself. For you to make yourself upset over him and his poor behavior is just plain neurotic."

"Me neurotic?" she fairly screamed as she jumped from the chair. "What about him? He's the craziest hoot I've ever met and he's getting worse all the time."

"I know he is. So why should you lose your mind over him? Since your church frowns on divorce, wouldn't you be so much better off if you could take him calmly and try to ignore his drinking and cursing?"

"After thirty years of his frittering the business down the drain and after thirty years of his deliberately start-

11

ing fights with me just so he'll have an excuse to leave the house and head for the bar, or to get out of making sexual advances to me, I should be sweet as apple pie and tell him it's all O.K.?"

"Not exactly. But that would get you calmed down and give you some relief from your migraine headaches. Since you can't change him, and I presume you can't because you've tried for a third of a century without success and he isn't even motivated enough even now to come to counseling with you, I would definitely say you might as well accept him as a drunk and relax."

This is the tone our previous sessions had taken: I trying to show her that she was getting herself angry over behavior her husband simply could not control and she always arguing with me that I just didn't understand her situation and that if I did I wouldn't talk like that.

But she was the mistaken one, not I. I had been through this debate with hundreds of people before, I knew almost word for word what their arguments would consist of, and I also knew they thought I was ridiculous for suggesting some of the views I did.

At such times I just grit my teeth and plow forward, hoping this session will be the one that brings sunshine to my client, a sunshine so bright that all the mental fog will be dispersed and he or she can finally see what I have been driving at for several sessions or several months of sessions.

Ms. Baker was no different than you, the reader, will be as you discover some of the latest psychological findings. These findings are so unusual your first reaction to them has to be denial. You will not be able to swallow all the advice I will give to help you overcome your hatred, resentment, or anger. Only after thinking about my advice for a long and hard time will you be able to use my counseling and make the new psychology work for you. Before that happens, however, you will simply go through the debating and questioning Ms. Baker went through.

Our sessions continued for another couple of weeks while I attempted to show her how she, not her husband, made her angry; what she could do to avoid and overcome that anger; and, lastly, how she could do this for almost every single annoyance she ever encountered, not just the frustrations of living with a drunk husband.

One day she came in all smiles. "You wouldn't believe what happened," she said with impatience.

"Mr. Baker called you a bad name and you laughed," was my guess.

"Yes, how did you know?" was her shocked response.

"Just a lucky hunch, that's all. Tell me what happened."

She took a breath and eagerly related the following: "If it hadn't happened to me I wouldn't have believed it. The other night my husband was working himself into a foul mood. He had come home from work, started drinking, and was getting more foulmouthed with every passing minute. At first I tried to ignore it, and for some minutes that helped. But as he kept up his badgering I couldn't ignore him and then began to feel myself getting hotter and hotter under the collar. I was just about to answer one of his sarcastic remarks when I remembered some of the things you had been telling me. You know: no one can anger me but myself; why get angry with him when he's so fouled up; forgive him for his nastiness and I'll do myself a big favor, and so on. Well, what happened then was beautiful, a miracle. I felt the tension and anger simply drain from my body. I could hardly believe how good I felt. There he stood, getting redder and redder in the face, expecting me to fire back the same thing he was throwing at me. Instead, I just sat down in my chair with a Mona Lisa smile on my face and let his anger roll off me like water off a duck.

"Now that I think of it, another reason I felt so good was that I realized I had not simply suppressed my anger and sat there with a lid on it. I've done that before, you know—pretend I wasn't angry but boiling up inside. This time I felt completely at peace because I had talked myself out of being angry, not just put it in a pressure cooker."

"And what happened to Mr. Baker?"

"Oh, him. He got madder and madder as I got calmer and calmer. Finally he put on his hat and, slamming the door behind him, went off to get drunk."

A year later I had occasion to speak with Ms. Baker again, this time about another family matter. Before she left my office I asked her how her husband was and how she had managed with her anger over the past many months. I was most gratified by what she said.

"My husband drinks as much as ever, even more, probably. He is losing the business, spending our savings, and will no doubt die from alcohol in the not-too-distant future. He's stopped fighting with me because I no longer play that game, thanks to you. I remind myself a hundred times a day that he is disturbed, that the poor dear can't help it, that it's an additional pity he won't even seek professional help, but that my getting upset over his neurosis won't help me or him. In the meantime I've made a life for myself. I attend church, play an active part in the hospital auxiliary, and attend my bridge parties every Wenesday afternoon. I'm lonely sometimes, of course. However, I'm at peace. Instead of having a frown on my face as I have had for the past thirty years, I now smile a great deal."

Exploding Myths About Anger

The true (but disguised) case of Ms. Baker is instructive in several important ways. In fact, it shoots holes into nine myths about anger, emotional disturbances, and psychotherapy.

MYTH No. 1: *People always learn from their experiences.*

If this had been true, then why was Ms. Baker reacting to her husband's baiting remarks in the same way after thirty years of marriage as she did the first year? Surely she must have told herself over and over: "I must be doing something wrong. I've tried fighting with him, arguing with him, showing him my anger, and none of this has ever changed him in the slightest." If people always learn from experience, she should then have evaluated her behavior, decided she wasn't getting anywhere, and come up with an entirely new approach. She did none of this. Perhaps for a period of time she might have tried being nice instead of angry when he was impossible, but there too she gave in too quickly and did not remain nice for a long enough time to let her new strategy work.

Something besides experience is needed to change behavior—not always, of course, but often. That something else was the advice I gave her during the six weeks I counseled with her. Most of this book will deal with that material in great detail so that you, the reader, can perhaps do for yourself what I was able to do for Ms. Baker.

Myth No. 2: *Old habits always require long periods of time to change.*

Such is clearly not true, as is shown in the case of Ms. Baker. According to this myth, a piece of behavior that has been practiced for thirty years should take at least one to three years to undo. The psychoanalysts in fact push that very notion: real change can come only by having therapy sessions for one hour, five or six times a week, for one to five years. At least that's what a great many of them have preached. Nonsense!

One of the reasons the vast majority of clients in psychoanalysis have taken huge sums and years of their lives to change (when they did) has been the ineffectiveness of the psychoanalytic method. Instead of its being the method of the elite and wealthy, it has been simply the only method available for decades that has had wide respectability, and it had the name of Sigmund Freud attached to it.

Don't be misled any longer! Psychoanalysis is dying—as it should. It had its day and must make way for better methods. The system of counseling that I will describe in this book is a tremendous advance over all the other therapies of the past because it is simple, effective, and quick in many, many instances. The newer psychology is able every now and then to make great changes in personality problems in as little as a single therapy session. Notice, I did not say "therapy hour." My individual sessions are now routinely thirty minutes long, my groups are sixty minutes long, and in both cases I am able to change long-standing habits in a single session or sometimes after several sessions despite the fact that the habits have existed for years. Most, of course, take longer—about six to twelve sessions thirty minutes long. Some people, it must be added, still take a year or two of fairly regular visits.

MYTH No. 3: *One cannot be undisturbed in a stressful environment.*

This is precisely what Ms. Baker thought. She was living with a disturbed and impossible man, so it was supposedly unthinkable for her to lead a normal life. What she did not know is that we make ourselves disturbed, and that if we learn how we do this we can also make ourselves undisturbed. Her husband gave her an endless series of *frustrations* throughout the years, but he never *disturbed* her with them. She did that.

In psychotherapy I taught her how she could remain stable even when he was neurotic. When she applied these insights to her own behavior she managed her emotions quite well even though the family scene was quite tense. Most people throughout the world have the mistaken belief that their feelings are created by others. In this book you will be shown how our neurotic feelings are really created, and how we create peace of mind. That this is possible was shown by Ms. Baker's gaining more and more calmness even though not a single element in her life had changed. A year after seeing me she was suffering from the same frustrations she had had for thirty years. However, she was not disturbing herself any longer. That new technique, that knowledge of how *not* to disturb herself, was the only major change in her life. And it was the only one really necessary to bring her relief.

Myth No. 4: *Everyone has a breaking point.*

If we're talking about shoving bamboo splinters under fingernails to make someone talk, sure, there's a breaking point. But in the vast majority of situations we ordinarily find ourselves in there is virtually no breaking point beyond which we cannot endure the nutty behavior of others. Again Ms. Baker was a case in point. Doubtlessly throughout her thirty years with Mr. Baker she must have thought many times she could not endure another quarrel with him. Yet she survived every ugly incident rather nicely and even fooled many of her friends about the true nature of her marital relationship. She contemplated suicide from time to time but never once attempted it.

After she terminated therapy, matters did not improve, they got worse. This time, instead of becoming more disturbed, she handled even his ruining the business with a calm she never believed possible. I am convinced she could have remained quite stable if her husband had died of cirrhosis of the liver or been thrown in jail for disorderly conduct.

When a person knows how, the limits of his endurance for frustration can be wondrous. I have known clients who had an incredible number of crises pile up on them in one week without causing them to blow their minds. Interestingly enough, the people who can tolerate these situations the best are sometimes the most neurotic. It's as though they have learned to live with frustrations and get used to them as some people get used to strong drink or poverty. I remember one fellow starting out his session by telling me about losing his job and then rapidly, for the next thirty minutes, reciting one sad happening after another that befell him just during the previous week. I sat with my mouth open as he went on and on, until I could hardly believe all these things had actually happened to one person in seven days. The whole business sounded so preposterous I just couldn't help bursting out laughing. I envisioned him as some poor joker walking through life with a little cloud over his head like a comic-strip character I saw years ago. He had a good laugh too when I apologized and explained my reaction to him.

MYTH No. 5: *Anger cannot be prevented, only suppressed.*

My client learned very much to her surprise she *could* actually avoid getting angry in the first place if she talked to herself correctly. She was not merely hiding her anger and pretending she wasn't angry, she really thought her way out of having any anger at all. Since it is we who talk ourselves into being mad, it is up to us to talk ourselves out of being mad.

No matter what the issue is, it is still possible to forgive your frustrater. I'm not now referring only to the normal and harmless reaction of raising your voice, arguing for your rights, feeling miffed, or even wanting to sock someone in the nose. These can be healthy and brief emotional reactions which cause no lasting damage to anyone.

The anger I am primarily referring to in this book is the kind that gets you into trouble, that eats your guts out, makes you act cruelly to others, or makes a complaining, whining baby out of you. These are the sick and dangerous emotions we must worry about, not the shouting matches or the occasional acts of firmness we must show our children. Technically these are angry emotions too and can be controlled and prevented in the same way the violent feelings can be prevented. It is simply not as urgent, however, to keep our voices down as it is to keep our hatreds down. And there is a distinction here. Raising your voice in an argument doesn't have to mean you hate the person you're arguing with. In fact, you frequently argue only with those you love, such as your parents, spouses, or children. If you didn't care for them, you'd show that by indifference, not a scolding.

Let us therefore not control all expressions of firmness or we will become colorless zombis. But the desire to kill, to seek a cruel revenge, to put someone down and want him to be hurt physically or emotionally—these can be thrown out completely, wiped out entirely until you can truly say you are not mad down deep.

MYTH No. 6: *Fight fire with fire.*

For all her married life Ms. Baker fought with her sick husband, stood up to him toe to toe, eyeball to eyeball, and nose tip to nose tip. Being a woman with a healthy sense of self-respect, she wasn't going to sit around and let anyone call her dirty names or accuse her of wrongs she never committed. If the jerk wanted a fight, she probably thought, I'll give him one. I'll make things so hot for him he'll learn never to pick on me unfairly again.

I could understand her taking such views if she had never tried them before. After all, until a strategy is used one never knows for certain just how it will work. What escapes me, however, is why she kept on with a strategy that seldom if ever worked. Not just day after day, week after week, or month after month, but literally year after year she used this same failing solution to her problems and almost always wound up more upset. Isn't it amazing how little we review our lives and examine what we're doing? Had Ms. Baker spent five minutes of serious thought about her behavior during those thirty years she would surely have concluded that her system was ineffective and that she had better change her methods.

The answer lies of course in the fact that she did not know what else to do. Once shown another (and more sensible) method for dealing with a hot head she was more than willing to try it and overthrow her old habits if the latter proved less efficient.

If you have had the philosophy of fight anger with anger, then you may get valuable instruction from this book, instruction you've probably been looking for these many years but have been unable to find. Read the following pages carefully, work hard at applying this new knowledge, and watch yourself cool off!

MYTH No. 7: *Both partners must be seen in marital counseling.*

Many couples in the middle of a marriage struggle never get their problems resolved because one of them thinks he or she knows more than a counselor, is afraid to talk to a professional because he or she might be found to be the most at fault, or is so neurotically sensitive that he or she wouldn't talk to a headshrinker lest friends think them weird.

In such instances, the husband or wife will usually call me up and ask how to get the spouse into marriage counseling. When I assure them this is not always necessary they sometimes believe me but sometimes do not. They seem to think both parties must agree to the counseling or therapeutic changes in the marriage are impossible. Agreed, this is very desirable but hardly necessary.

21

In the case of Ms. Baker a significant change was made in her marriage even though I never once saw or even talked to Mr. Baker personally or by phone. Granted I might have helped the marriage more had I been given the opportunity to work with the husband as well. However, there was absolutely no reason not to proceed with counseling his wife just because he wouldn't join in. She at least gained peace of mind, though he continued to go downhill.

MYTH No. 8: *The "real reasons" behind a problem—the hidden causes from childhood—must be understood before personality changes can be made.*

In the six or so sessions I had with Ms. Baker there was no time to delve deeply into her long past and search out all the minute childhood happenings that might explain why she would marry an alcoholic, why she would accept so much abuse from him, and why she would stick with him rather than leave him. Maybe she was chronically angry with her father, who might have been a dependent man, and maybe a lot of other things. Actually, in most instances it really isn't necessary to understand a great deal about a person's past and in many instances absolutely nothing need be known to still allow the possibility of great changes.

In the few sessions I had with Ms. Baker I don't recall digging up her past, only her present. I wanted to know what she was angry about currently, and then I told her how she was making herself furious with her man and making matters worse. I could have shown her where she developed the angry habits, but that wasn't as important as showing her how she was getting herself steamed up *today*, with *this* man, over *that* issue.

The only times I have found it necessary to go into

historical detail with a client are when he is really foggy about his feelings and memories. In those cases he needs to get his bearings, and going into his background can be important to getting that done. Most people, fortunately, can describe their problems fairly clearly and can even give you a pretty good theory of what is causing their disturbances. In those cases it is hardly necessary to be a psychological Sherlock Holmes. Just teach them what they need to know about their present upset and how to avoid future ones.

Therefore, if you have emotional problems and doubt that I can explore your background by means of a book, you're right. Instead, take heart from the exploding of this myth and stop believing I need to understand when you first burped or when you got your first black eye. Ninety-five percent of you need only to know what's going on now, not what went on years ago.

MYTH No. 9: *Angry people are mentally ill and need treatment.*

Ms. Baker was as normal as you or I. The fact that she and her husband tangled horns all those years actually proves this. Who would have done differently under those conditions?

"But," you will protest, "wasn't she pretty upset and mentally ill on many occasions because of that problem with her husband?"

Of course she was upset, but since when does that mean she'd have to be mentally ill? All of us are upset fairly frequently, yet we wouldn't call ourselves mentally ill. I like to reserve the term "illness" for people who really do have something wrong with their brains, such as a senile person because of hardening of the arteries, or a brain-damaged person hurt in a fall or car accident.

23

Germs such as those causing syphilis can also cause actual damage to the brain. These are the people suffering from mental illness. The rest of the population that is upset but yet have intact brains are that way because they were trained to be upset. That's right, we were all taught to think in emotionally upsetting ways when frustrated. We aren't ill, just misinformed!

Anger is one of the most commonly taught emotional reactions. Fear and anger have to be the most common, and I'm not sure which comes first. It really doesn't matter anyway, because whether first or second there's a whale of a lot of it around.

Nothing in Ms. Baker's behavior suggested she had anything wrong with her brain, just the habits she had learned. So I proceeded to teach her to think differently. I then assumed the role of a teacher while she took the role of a student; my office became a classroom; her therapy session became a lesson during which I assigned her homework. Although she didn't know it at first, she was being helped over her emotional hang-ups in the same way she would have been helped by a bridge teacher, a dancing instructor, or her golf pro.

Doing away with anger is a habit one must learn. Psychotherapists can now teach this subject with the same degree of precision, common sense, and speed as most skills are learned. That's what it is, this business of not being angry, a learned skill. It is a new habit the client acquires when he knows (a) how he disturbed himself and (b) how he can get himself out of being angry.

Read On and Cool Off

What happened to Ms. Baker has happened to hundreds of other clients once they were shown how to think differently. In the following pages you will be informed of the latest psychological findings on the subjects of anger, resentment, fury, and hate, and how to control and rid yourself of all of them. Your life can change enormously by making you more easygoing, nicer to be with, and more patient, and you will be helped in your role as parent, spouse, or worker. Too many people have every reason for success in this life, but because they fly off the handle so quickly never make the grade. I well remember a radio operator, a young fellow, newly married and the father of one child, who had several jobs every year because he was a hothead. Whenever he was given an order by his boss he would bristle with supersensitivity and soon walk off in a huff. Maybe he'd go home and boast that he wouldn't let anyone push him around. How he thought he'd pay the rent that month escapes me.

What he needed to know was how to let things roll off his back, how not to make insults out of harmless comments, and how to be firm without also being angry. These are the goals of this book. Read on! Many of you will learn enough just from the following pages to make enormous changes in your angry behavior. Those who cannot gain complete control from reading will at least know the fundamentals of emotional control and can then get counseling and do the job in much less time than would otherwise be required.

Before we get into the specific techniques of controlling anger, I think it would be wise first to talk a little about *why* it is better to control anger. Until you see what I mean by anger and what it can do to you, the motivation to avoid all anger will not be there. You see, I regard all anger as neurotic if it hurts you or others needlessly.

2

Should We Avoid All Anger?

Ninety-nine percent of the time I'd say yes. Why? Because it hurts when I get mad. I may get a headache, a stomach spasm, a foul mood which ruins my appetite, and so on. So why should I want an emotional reaction that could do that to me?

What I want most out of life is happiness, pleasure, and contentment, not pain or displeasure. Remaining calm and patient about my frustrations will guarantee me the greatest peace of mind. Getting angry over not getting my way will often not remove the frustration and will distress me on top of it. Neither you nor I can be deeply or chronically mad without paying the price for it, that is, being pained.

Some Harmful Consequences of Anger

1. *Anger almost always increases your frustrations.* This is the last thing you want to happen because being initially frustrated is unpleasant enough. To *add* to the frustration someone else is giving you is just not sensible. For example, the wife who resents her husband's coming home late for dinner and who gives him a tongue-lashing for letting her lovely supper be spoiled may make

matters infinitely worse by accusing him of being unfaithful. By hitting below the belt she gets a brief period of sweet revenge, but when he wheels about and leaves the house for an all-night drinking spree at the local bar, what has she gained? Wouldn't she have thought his coming home late was frustrating enough? But now, after suffering with the spoiled dinner, she has unwittingly devised a plan whereby she will suffer from *two* frustrations rather than one.

If this situation stopped there, it wouldn't be so bad. However, getting angry at someone usually doesn't cause you just one additional frustration, it causes many. In the case of the tardy husband it is easy to speculate how many additional acts of revenge he could cook up to get back at his wife. We've already seen how he might get drunk to punish her. But have you thought of the money he would spend in getting drunk and how his wife might have counted on it desperately? He might subconsciously want to get arrested or injured to further aggravate his wife, and lastly, he might find it hard to forget and forgive her for her attack on him, and this could give him reason enough to ignore her, yell at her, or put her down a thousand times until he got over his mad.

It may sound as though I'd recommend kowtowing to this husband, but this is not true. In another chapter I will give a number of pointers on handling this sort of obstinate and vengeful behavior.

2. *Getting angry prevents you from solving problems.* Anger is, after all, not a solution to a frustration. It is a reaction to frustration. To make your boss get off your back requires that you work harder, be more pleasant to him, or get another job. Getting angry with him will give him the best excuse in the world to fire you, or at the

very least to continue to annoy you greatly.

Being hateful simply fills your thoughts with delicious ways of getting even with others, not with how to get others to behave differently toward you. It frequently happens that those who are angry all the time also have the most problems. This is not accidental, it is a result of their chronic anger. Instead of trying to douse a fire with gasoline, use water. Instead of getting people to treat you more fairly by being hostile, cool your resentment and take the time to figure out how you might make a friend out of an enemy. This is admittedly a difficult task and it requires intense concentration and imagination. Being angry simply prevents those traits from entering your thinking. The net result is that things get worse and worse as you become angrier and angrier.

Another technical point to remember about punishment is that it teaches the wrongdoer only one thing: what *not* to do. It does not teach him the wise thing to do. These are two separate tasks and must be accomplished by firmness on the one hand and instructions on how to do a job correctly on the other hand. Yelling at your daughter for cramming the dishwasher does not show her how to stack dishes safely. Your son who gets boxed on the ears because he mowed the lawn sloppily has not automatically learned how to mow it neatly. To do that his father would have to take him step by step, show him how to clip the edges, how to mow under the hedges, how to bag the grass in plastic bags, and so on. Merely scolding him doesn't achieve these ends.

3. *You set a poor example of mental health.* Have you ever noticed how much of your behavior is copied from others? Your clothing styles are perhaps the most obvious examples. It usually doesn't matter what you think

28

about cuffs on the pants, if enough of your friends are wearing cuffs you will soon be doing the same. The fashion industry relies completely on the masses' following the examples set by the pacesetters. When the First Lady goes somewhere without a hat, the nation follows. The examples are so numerous that proof is not needed to sustain this point.

What is not so generally appreciated is the degree to which we copy people's *behavior*. If a movie star has an illegitimate baby, you can bet your last teething ring thousands of knuckleheaded teen-agers are going to worship their screen goddess by offering her their own illegitimate offspring. When a famous person attempts or succeeds at suicide, the suicide rate in the nation takes a big jump.

In short, we seem to be directed by the actions of others more than we generally appreciate. The way you act can have an enormous influence on those around you. If you act like a tough hood and run a street gang, you can be sure all the kids under you will set you up as their idol and do whatever followers do to get the approval of the big man. But if you had the respect of a gang of fellows and denounced violence, you might just be surprised at how many fellows would honor you and try to stand up against those street organizations.

Anger is one of those emotions which are especially infectious. When one person wants to act aggressively it doesn't take much to instill that feeling in those watching that aggression. Should the husband scold the waiter for poor service, the wife is also likely to feel indignant and abused. One person's anger works on the other's so that the combined angers become multiplied rather than merely added. This is why a mob is such a dangerous social group. Each person is feeding the hatred of the next, each one feels pressed to copy the example of the other, and the net result of this emotional buildup is behavior most of them would never dream of doing individually. For example, how many of us could cut off a man's penis because he raped a local teen-ager, stuff it in his mouth, cut his belly open, and then drag him through the streets by his feet? I suggest such animal-like behavior would be near impossible for 99 percent of us. But this actually happened in a small peaceful town in our land when the 99 percent followed the example of the vicious 1 percent.

To increase the mental health of those around you, to decrease the violence in your home and on your job, and to make this the kind of world you would enjoy living in, become a healthy, unangry person yourself. Not only do you thereby subtract the anger you could have added, you also diminish all the hate and anger other people would have added who are following your superior example.

4. *Anger can make you physically sick.* The next time you hear someone arguing in a raised voice, try to imagine what is happening in his lungs, around his lungs, and at the farthest ends of his body. Blood pressure builds up. A weak heart can be strained to a dangerous point. Headaches often follow the buildup of suppressed rage. The whole internal physiological system is strained, ready for an emergency, and the whole digestive process is shut off or slowed down. I've known several clients who swore they were telling me the truth when they said they had been so angry they went temporarily blind. Stomachaches, indigestion, colitis, and all sorts of disturbances to the digestive and alimentary tracts can arise from chronic anger. You can turn

red, perspire, tremble, and be very uncomfortable, all because you are hateful, mad, wrathful, bitter, or angry.

As if the damage to your body weren't enough, stop and think of the many ways in which you can become neurotic or psychotic because of anger. The paranoid would not be in that condition if he could forgive people their faults and transgressions. Many alcoholics would never drink nearly so much as they do if they weren't so angry and upset over the frustrations in their lives. Millions of marriages would have been saved if one or both partners could have kept their mouths shut when one mate was feeling disturbed. And lastly, most of the people rotting in our jails are there because they couldn't control their tempers.

I can't think of a single human emotion that is more dangerous to each of us than anger. That more hasn't been written about it is simply amazing. Now, feeling very comfortable with the subject, I can offer an explanation as to why it has frightened off the writers. The answer? It was too simple. That's right—understanding anger finally turns out not to be a difficult and complex thing after all. It boils down to two irrational beliefs: one, you must have your way, and two, people are bad and should be severely dealt with if they behave wrongly.

5. *Anger is the greatest single cause for divorce.* It isn't money, sex, in-laws, jealousy, jobs, coming home late, other men, other women, or any of dozens of other frustrations that strain marriages. It is purely and simply the *getting angry* over these conditions. If the couple would not get angry, moody, give each other the cold shoulder, become spiteful, and certainly if they would not use physical force against each other, most marriages could survive very nicely. Then the majority of divorces

would occur only in the marriages where there has really been a serious mismating in the first place. Choosing your partner foolishly is certainly possible and may lead to divorce. Many marriages, however, are begun by people who are deeply in love, who are suited to each other as they would probably be to most people, and who should stay together if at all possible. The single most disastrous cause for their breaking up is their childish behavior when they don't get what they want.

We must learn that frustrations are a part of life. They are as inevitable as death. You could no more be alive and not have frustrations than you could be alive and not eat. More importantly, you can no more live with someone and not be frustrated by him several times during the day than you could read a book without turning the pages. It matters not how well you get along with the people around you, or how much you and they love each other. They will frustrate you whether they plan it or not. It simply cannot be helped some of the time.

For you to get angry with your loved ones because they are frustrating you is like being angry with them because they breathe. I know you wouldn't really be that foolish, but with frustrations you are. You think people you love should never frustrate you! What rubbish! It is the people you love the most who frustrate you in special ways. Why? Because the persons you don't care for can more easily be ignored.

Learning to accept frustrations philosophically is one answer to a harmonious marriage. Where they can be changed, fine. When they cannot be changed, resign yourself to them calmly. Don't split a gut over them and create a super frustration such as a fight or series of fights that may lead to a divorce.

6. *Anger is responsible for one of the most depraved of all human behaviors: child abuse.* This is truly one of the saddest of our human weaknesses. Sometimes parents lose patience with their babies for completely conscious reasons—the child cried all night, it restricted the young mother to her apartment days on end, it cost the parents large sums of money in medical bills, etc. When they strike out at the child they are fully aware of the frustrations involved in their anger. At other times parents can punish their children for subconscious reasons: the baby represents the mother herself, and if the mother beats her baby she is symbolically beating herself when she was a little girl and behaved badly. Or perhaps the baby represents one's brother or sister of whom one was very jealous. By beating the child the sibling of childhood is being punished.

Whether for conscious or unconscious reasons, and whether for the above reasons or others which were not mentioned, the common denominator to all this pathetic behavior is anger. If parents would learn how not to be angry over a crying baby, being penned up in an apartment, hating oneself or one's brother or sister as a child, much of this child abuse would never occur.

And just think for one moment of the damage you might be causing future generations by such behavior. What will your child be like when he is grown and has children of his own if you beat him daily? What kind of adult will that baby be if you lose so much control that you pick him up bodily and throw him against the wall? And when you really let yourself go and chain the child to his bed, or burn him with cigarettes, or starve him (all of which have actually happened), what kind of people are we supposed to get from these treatments?

Are There Benefits from Anger?

From what I have been saying you're likely to get the impression that all anger is bad, that no one should ever speak up with indignation, and that you must always be in perfect control of your feelings or else you're neurotic. You're right and you're wrong. Confusion comes from misunderstanding anger and firmness.

When you're angry you want to make someone stop doing something he's doing (such as picking on you), or begin doing something for which he is responsible (such as helping with the dishes instead of watching TV). In addition, however, you are prepared to hurt that person if he doesn't go along with you.

Firmness, on the other hand, has to do with getting people to start or stop certain behavior without having the desire to hurt them if they don't agree with you. This means that all anger is neurotic because it either hurts you or someone else needlessly. I understand, of course, that many of our minor angry reactions, though neurotic by my definition, are not serious and need not be guarded against in most cases. Throughout this book I am most concerned with those angry conditions which hurt you a great deal or hurt others a great deal. But from a theoretical point of view I want to be sure we understand each other when I insist that all resentments, all angers, all hostilities are neurotic unless they arise from self-defense. I don't mean all kinds of defense either, just physical self-defense. If someone is cursing you up one side and down the other, there is no need for you to defend yourself since that's a psychological attack and won't hurt you. If someone wants to use your face for a punching bag, however, you'd be a fool if you didn't defend yourself. Notice, I did not say that you should first get angry and *then* defend yourself. It is perfectly possible (with training) to react fairly calmly to people's frustrations first and then beat the tar out of them if you need to.

From a practical point of view we all know that anger and hostility often pay off handsomely whether they're neurotic reactions or not. Soldiers often fight better when boiling mad, the underworld controls its territory through violence, and the fellow who doesn't mind swinging his fists at the slightest hint of an insult probably doesn't get insulted very often. True, he may have an occasional migraine headache or high blood pressure (neurotic conditions which he has created as a result of his anger), but little he probably cares. He gets respect, feels safe, and may not mind having to pay for these benefits with a headache or heart pain. But just imagine how much better he would be if he could be firm and not angry.

In short, what the healthy person cultivates is the habit of being assertive, not hostile. Assertiveness means to stand up for your rights in a nonviolent way *if possible*. Hostility means to stand up for yourself *and* to be angry. The former is a wonderful habit to get into if you can do it. But if you can't for the time being, it may still do you more good to be hostile and angry than to be weak and passive and take all sorts of abuse from others.

Take the case of Bob and his very submissive wife. Years ago she talked him into changing jobs and it later seemed like an unwise move. Bob became increasingly distant toward her and practically forgot why he devel-

35

oped these feelings. It was only after several years had passed and they were on the verge of divorce that he recalled how miffed he was with her for interfering in his decision to stay with his previous employer because he could easily have risen in the ranks, something he was not able to manage in the new job.

Sue didn't know what was wrong but didn't say much about the way she was treated. In fact, she put up with so much of his abuse over the years that he began to lose respect for her for *that* as much as for her urging him to make that wrong move. Finally things got so bad between them that he sought other women, wouldn't talk to her, and finally didn't want to stay married any longer.

One of the major complaints Bob had about his wife was the abuse she took from him. He said to me during one of his therapy sessions: "I can't stand having a slave for a wife. I want a human being who won't agree with me one hundred percent."

It was apparent to me that Sue might have saved her marriage had she spoken up to Bob, told him to cut out his nonsense and stop blaming her for one mistake after three years, and to shape up or ship out. I would have hoped she could have done this unangrily but firmly. That might have worked wonders. Assuming, however, she didn't know how to do that, then she would still have been infinitely better off screaming at him, having a few ugly scenes, losing her appetite a few days, or not sleeping well for a period of time. Those conditions would have passed, the air would have cleared, and Bob would have found a new sense of respect for his wife. These would have been neurotic reactions to be sure, but so what? The payoff would have been well worth the momentary discomfort.

So you see I do not want to be rigid about getting angry. If you do not know how to be firm without being angry, then by all means get sore and be firm. Being firm and assertive with people who are doing you wrong is terribly important if you are ever to be happy. However, you will be even happier if you learn (we hope through reading the following chapters) how to be firm, assertive, and *un*angry.

Acting Angry

Fully realizing that anger is a condition that often commands much respect, it would be a shame not to take advantage of this feature. But how can you do this and still live peacefully inside? By *making believe* you're furious and ready to explode, that's how. Act as if you're sore but be forgiving and understanding down deep inside. And where and when is it wise to do this? I can think of several general situations where acting angry rather than feeling angry actually makes sense.

Suppose you're in a hurry but the kids are dawdling. You're in the car with the engine running, you're already a bit late, and the family doesn't seem to appreciate this. Calmly telling them to move along may well fall on deaf ears, so the only sensible thing to do is yell.

"Hurry up, you kids, or I'll go to the movie alone. I hate to be kept waiting."

This and a few other growling utterances can easily make the kids move in ways they simply won't if they don't think the issue is urgent. And the whole scene can be done deliberately, with inner calm, while looking like a bear on the outside. All you have to do is remind yourself that it's not going to kill anyone if you are late for the show, kids will be kids and occasionally need hustling, and a little pressure once in a while really won't hurt them.

There are actually numerous times in a month when a gruff voice and a few well-chosen words cut right to the heart of things and make wheels spin. You must be careful, however, not to make this habitual. Use it sparingly because the family or the employees won't be able to tell that you aren't actually angry and they'll become fearful, resentful, or spiteful. At that point your strategy will have backfired. Then you may find yourself not pretending to be angry anymore—you *will* be angry.

Is Anger or Violence Ever Justified?

In addition to the typical situations just mentioned when anger can be a healthy reaction (if not overdone), there is only one condition I can think of when violence is justified: self-defense. You may want to turn the other cheek when taking a beating but I prefer to punch the other fellow's cheek. I have only one life to give to myself, and I'd be a fool not to fight for it if someone threatened it. Murder in self-defense has been declared legal by the courts. I'm convinced a great deal of misery in the lives of many people I have counseled would not have occurred if the victims had not been so hesitant to stand up for themselves, even if that meant being violent.

Women seem more often than men to be the victims of violence. A woman who regularly takes a beating from her husband and doesn't do anything to fight back is taking her life in her hands. Some of these poor creatures have been ruined for life because they were so frightened for their lives. When not wanting to submit to their husband's sexual advances, they were beaten until they did. Some wound up with numerous children they couldn't raise and eventually had to turn them over to the state for rearing. During those years of torment these women lived in constant fear, and their children practically all developed serious personality problems. What they got in the end was worse than anything they might have received had they stood up to their sick husbands.

Do weak females have real protection against violent husbands? You bet they do! One woman—this is a true story—waited until her spouse fell asleep and then conked him over the head with the heel of his shoe. She got a beating for this, but that night she waited until he fell asleep again and once more he had his dreams turned rudely into nightmares. By using his head as a drum she made him so jittery about falling asleep he began to let up on her. The fact that nothing seemed to stop her gave him the uneasy feeling his wife was off her rocker and might stab him while he slept. She did nothing to dispel this notion. Soon he changed in his violent ways and merely yelled, something she could manage as well as he.

Whether she defended herself with hatred in her heart is not so important as the fact that she *did* defend herself. She might have spared herself the additional distress of being angry, but at least she wasn't passive and continuing to take his unfair abuse. Defending herself for her very life far outshadowed the question of whether she did it neurotically or rationally.

Another way the weak can defend themselves against an unreasonable family or neighbors is to send the police after them or, if they are seriously disturbed persons, commit them to a state hospital. This might bring on

39

more violence, but that would come even if they did not report them to the police or commit them. Only by being firm, by standing up to violent people, do they get the idea that violence causes them more distress than it's worth.

In the final analysis *you are dominated because you have allowed it*. No one can always make you give in to him, even by force, unless you happen to be in a concentration camp and want to live. If you don't want to live any longer, you could tell your jailer to go to hell and let him shoot you rather than make you walk barefooted in the snow or do all manner of inhuman things. The choice is yours. In most instances such drastic alternatives are not in question. Children and women do not need to tolerate physical threat if they will accept different homes, divorce, living off welfare, giving up jobs they otherwise like, and so on. These are usually great prices to pay, but their lives and dignity are in the balance and well worth the price.

Often a person will not stand up for himself, because he believes his issue is unimportant and he is afraid to take a firm stand. The fact that he is upset over it and seeing me still may not convince him the matter is worth making a fuss over. These are usually poor excuses by persons with little self-esteem who think every cause is righteous but their own. They lack that healthy spark of selfishness which makes people put their desires before the concerns of others a fair share of the time.

When they pigheadedly insist they cannot stand up to a bully or a dominating parent I ask them to consider a situation they would feel strong enough to face. For instance, one young fellow who was quite dominated by his mother over every major expenditure was so angry at her he was afraid he'd hurt her feelings if he told her to leave him and his wife alone. I insisted that he could very well tell her off nicely and settle the matter if he thought it was important enough. For example, if mother insisted that he sell his house tomorrow would he do so? No? Then why couldn't he stand up to her in regard to her dictating his financial affairs to him?

If his mother insisted he sell his children and murder his wife, would he do so merely to avoid disappointing her? No? Then apparently he *was* fully capable of standing up for himself *if* he felt the issue was important enough. Well, wasn't it important enough to him to run his own life? Yes? Then what was he waiting for? Surely he *could* stand up for himself in that respect if he could easily do it in so many other respects.

3

Who Makes You Mad? You Do!

SOME PEOPLE CAN DISCOVER THE SECRET OF ANGER ALL by themselves. Unfortunately these are only a few. One of these I remember quite well was a woman who, when she was yet a teen-ager, had this experience.

"I used to have a very bad temper. I was always fighting and I don't even know over what. Once I had a two-month running argument with my father. Then one day I decided the whole thing was just a childish piece of behavior on my part and that I would not let myself get angry again as long as I lived. With a few exceptions I have kept that pledge.

"My husband was very bothered by my never getting mad and would sometimes try to infuriate me so much that I would have to act angry just to get him off my back. All the time, however, even when he broke my arm and put me in the hospital to provoke my anger, I didn't feel any. I thought he was a dumb sap who didn't know better and I wasn't about to let him bring me down to being the sort of person I had been as an adolescent."

This is truly a remarkable confession and clearly shows how anger is controllable without counseling, for years, under great temptation. Those of you who cannot achieve this degree of insight will want to study this chapter very thoroughly a number of times.

To get over being angry you must first get over the idea you have been taught all your life, namely, that *other people make you angry*. Someone called you lazy and you think that made you mad. Your best friend forgot to repay the money he borrowed from you and you think that made you mad. In every case I come across, whether male or female, adult or child, the belief is always the same: other people or events can upset you and make you resentful, angry, or even furious. This is not accurately what happens when we become disturbed.

If others do not upset us, then how *do* we become angry? By thinking angrily about the things that happen to us, that's how.

"Do you mean to tell me," you might be asking right now, "that I never get angry because of what someone else has done, that I always cause my own anger?"

Yes, that's exactly what I mean. If you did not think angry thoughts you could not get angry. It's that simple to explain, but not to do.

"But," you may still ask, "what sort of things would I be telling myself that would make me angry?"

The Complete Sequence of Getting Angry

From beginning to end there are either five or six steps in getting mad. If you end the sequence with merely feeling angry and wanting to kill someone, you will stop at step five and not go to the sixth. If you wind up punishing rather than penalizing someone, you've gone all the way to the sixth and final step.

For the sake of clarity the whole process of getting angry, resentful, mad, or furious will be explained below, but always bear in mind that these six steps are

43

easily condensed into only two steps: (1) I *want* my way, and (2) I *must* therefore have it.

Step one: *"I want something."*

We all have millions of desires and wishes. I want love, wealth, fair treatment, respect, safety, and I also want to fly to the moon, to be king of the world, own all of California, and live forever. I could go on and on with all the things I want, and you could too. Daydreaming is one of the nice pastimes that help idle away boring days and, if not carried to extremes, will not get us admitted to a state hospital.

Man's wants are literally as vast as his imagination. They are the source of all invention, charity, knowledge, and art. That something so good could be distorted by neurotic minds to end up so vicious and destructive has to be one of the major tragedies of life.

Step two: *"I didn't get what I wanted and am frustrated."*

The wish has been denied, as of course many of them had to be. Of all the desires we have, only the smallest fraction of them are ever fulfilled. This too is one of the unavoidable regrets man must live with.

The wise man knows life cannot give him all he wants, so he is content with all he can gain through hard work or luck. He accepts philosophically what he cannot get even after striving for it. He is frustrated but not angry. He wanted something. He did not get it.

What he does about this frustration is extremely important in determining the direction his emotions now take. Step three is the first point at which you can begin to react neurotically.

Step three: *"It is awful and terrible not to get what I want."*

If you define your frustration as a catastrophe, you've

44

had it. At this point, depending on what you tell yourself about your frustration, you can develop several different kinds of neuroses. If you believe a certain set of ideas, you could easily become depressed instead of angry. Depression is brought about by your thinking (*a*) you are a worthless person because you did something bad, or (*b*) you ought to feel sorry for yourself because you are frustrated, or (*c*) you should pity someone else. These are the three ways you can get depressed over your not getting your way.

But you can also become very fearful instead. However, the thoughts you must believe to become anxious at this step are quite different from those you must believe if you are to become depressed. To become afraid you must (*a*) believe persons and events can literally upset you, and (*b*) think constantly about anything that might prove difficult or dangerous. Phobias, anxieties, and other forms of fear such as shyness, timidity, and withdrawal come from these two neurotic beliefs.

A third, but by no means last, set of emotional reactions you could have are the hateful ones: anger, fury, revenge, and spitefulness. Once again, however, the sentences you would tell yourself to produce these feelings are quite different from those you have to think to produce depression or fear. Briefly, they are: (*a*) I must have my way and it is awful not to get everything I want, and (*b*) you are wicked for frustrating me and deserve to be punished. It may have escaped you that I have been describing emotional disturbances not by frustrating events, but by the statements we make to ourselves *about* these frustrations. The latest psychological findings are showing us that we become upset by *thinking* in upsetting ways, not by encountering frustrating situations. In other words, depressing thoughts bring on depressed feelings, scary thoughts make you feel afraid, and thinking angry and punishing thoughts brings on angry and vengeful feelings.

In case you don't get the full impact of these statements, then consider this: once you have reached the age of reason (about early adolescence) you are the only person upsetting you. Since that time of your life no one has made you depressed, jealous, scared, angry, or directly upset in any way. You've done that by having irrational ideas which create those feelings. To change these neurotic emotions into healthy and painless feelings you must stop believing those ideas which create anger, depression, or fear in the first place. For instance, if you do not believe in ghosts, you obviously cannot be afraid of them. And if you do not believe it is terrible not to get what you want, then you can never really get angry over being frustrated.

"But," you may protest, "suppose I want something that really would be horrible to be without, such as food, wouldn't I be sensible and healthy to get upset and angry then?"

No, not necessarily, would be my reply. If getting furious will get you the food you need to live, then get furious. To do anything less would be ridiculous. But suppose you were in a concentration camp and were slowly starving to death. Demanding larger rations from your sadistic guard could very likely be the end of your worries. In that case you would very wisely tell yourself that you don't need more food, that what you have will let you live for months (even though you'll look like a skeleton), and that making waves could bug your captors so much they wouldn't hesitate to shoot you and be rid of a pest.

Fortunately most of the frustrations we deal with daily are not of such serious nature. Most of the time the things we gripe about are little concerns, such as a car not working when we have to be somewhere, the kids taking their sweet time about getting to bed, your not being able to find the hammer when you go to hang up a picture, and so on.

None of these situations could provoke us to anger if we could convince ourselves we did not have to have our way and that being frustrated was not awful.

To remain unangry throughout your life you had better learn to question the idea that not getting your way is unbearable and *must* lead to a disturbance. If you can beat that nutty idea into the ground, you'll be a more stable person for it.

Step three is the first step at which you will generally become disturbed. Step four, however, always leads specifically to anger.

Step four: *"You shouldn't frustrate me! I must have my way."*

Now you're asking to get angry. You wanted something and didn't get it. That was merely healthy wishing. At this point, however, you've changed that wish into a demand and that's bad. If you get what you demand, everything will of course be peachy creamy. But if you do not get what you think you need, you will think you are being so deprived that the sky will fall in, and you'll just have to get mad and indignant over such a monstrous unfairness.

Perhaps you don't deserve to be frustrated because you've always paid your club dues and walked old ladies across the street. But why shouldn't you be denied what you deserve? This world never was nor ever will be run completely by just standards. The people who

47

dish out the justice are as human as you and I, so how can we seriously expect nonfrustrating behavior from them?

Furthermore, when you insist others should not frustrate you, do you realize how dictatorial you're being? Where do you get off telling everyone and his brother what they can or cannot do? Since when do you have control over me? If I want to frustrate you, why don't I have that right? Even if you tell me I would be breaking a legal or moral code, you still have no right to insist I cannot be a lawbreaker. If I want to speed past your house and risk being given a ticket, you have no moral right to insist I should not speed past your house. That's my business and my problem. And if I don't mind being a screwball, then do what you can about getting me arrested or hospitalized, but don't tell me I can't act badly.

Step five: *"You're bad for frustrating me."*

Now we get into the really dangerous part of this series. Until now you've been only angry, but not necessarily hateful or vengeful. With step five, however, you've made one of the most unfortunate evaluations of someone else you could possibly make. You have said someone was bad because he or she frustrated you, and you've implied that if someone is bad, he is also worthless, evil, and wicked—that he and his behavior are the same.

"Well," you will ask, "aren't people and their behavior the same? Surely we can't separate a person from his actions, can we?"

Yes we can. I am *not* my behavior. I refuse to think of myself as a human being by *how* I act. My actions might be objectionable, but that never means I should reject myself because I reject my actions. I can sensibly reject all sorts of features about myself without thinking I'm no good. I can dislike my possessions, such as my shirt, shoes, or hat without thinking that I too am no good. But I can go farther than material things. I can even separate my physical attributes from me as a whole human being. For instance, I can reject the shape of my head without thinking that I am bad. I can dislike the shape of my nose and still believe I am not worthless as a person.

And I can even carry this example farther, into my personality and character. Why can't I disapprove of my laziness, cowardice, or dishonesty and still accept myself? Must I hate myself completely because I cheat or take advantage of others? Unless I forgive myself for these imperfections I shall most certainly become depressed. And if I cannot accept you with your faults, I will reject you and your behavior. I will become angry at you because I've decided you have to be bad simply because there are certain characteristics you have that are offensive (a sloppy suit), or physical features I find ugly (your bad teeth), or your behavior is irritating (you brag). In each case, however, I can most certainly separate the suit, the bad teeth, and your bragging from you as a person and dislike the former without disliking or, worse, hating the latter.

You are after all much more than a clean suit, clean teeth, and a modest fellow. You are a person who can always accept himself. If your sloppy suit offends your boss who runs a haberdashery store, then it makes sense for him and you to believe that you are valueless to him as a *salesman*. Not being an acceptable salesman because you dress poorly certainly cannot mean anything more than that: you are unacceptable as a salesman. Why, however, can't you be perfectly important to yourself or others if you don't dress well? This hardly means others cannot accept you, even if you could not accept yourself. In the final analysis, however, accepting yourself with your shortcomings is the most important act you can perform in your own behalf, for without it you condemn yourself for being imperfect.

There are three reasons people act badly for which they are not required to be blamed: stupidity, ignorance, and disturbance. In the case of stupidity we are talking about someone with limited intelligence or skill. If your child is mentally slow, you certainly wouldn't blame him for all the poor grades he brings home because you'd know he couldn't help it. We can dislike and disapprove his poor grades and still accept the child, can't we?

Now suppose you enroll your daughter in the local ballet class and after several months it appears she has the grace of a limping camel. Would you be angry with her? You'd have to be very unfeeling and unthinking to do so. Your daughter's dancing is bad but she certainly isn't. She dances badly because she is stupid in the subject (just doesn't have what it takes), just as the boy in the previous example does not have what it takes in school subjects. If you asked me to compose a symphony, I would have to plead stupidity because not only do I not know enough about music but I just can't come up with all those melodies!

Ignorance is the second reason why we frequently behave badly but for which we need not be blamed. How can you possibly be held responsible for not being able to perform acts you were never taught? The mechanic who fixes your car but does it incorrectly and thereby causes you an expensive accident is still an acceptable person although he is not a worthwhile mechanic. If he was not taught to work on your particular car model, there is no way we can blame him for doing badly. We can of course hold him responsible for taking on assignments he was not trained for and perhaps fire him for poor judgment. To believe that he is bad because he is a bad mechanic or a poor judge of his own skills, however, is totally unfounded.

The last reason people behave badly but should not be blamed for doing so is their emotional disturbances. In this case the person is not unintelligent or unskilled, nor is he ignorant. But this doesn't make any difference. He does the bad deed even though he'll hang for it. He yells at his kids ten thousand times, even though he can see as well as you or I that yelling has never accomplished anything. He still gives his wife the third degree whenever she is late three minutes even though he knows his jealousy is driving her away more each time he accuses her of running around.

The emotionally disturbed person cannot help acting like a neurotic. If he could help it, he wouldn't perform like one. The tragedy of the whole situation is precisely that he knows how he is hurting himself and those he loves but he just can't stop acting like a fool. To understand him we must not blame him for his foolish behavior but must forgive him instead. He does not want to be such a jerk about his behavior any more than others want him to be one. He behaves as he does not because he is evil, but because he was trained to behave like that.

For instance, the jealous husband who is driving his wife into the arms of other men was taught that his importance in life depends upon his wife's loving him above all other men. He also believes he will be insulted and humiliated if he is rejected for another man. He was taught that he is only as valuable as others say he is.

Should his wife reject him, that would be proof of his nothingness.

Anyone raised with these sets of false notions is bound to be disturbed if his wife dances with another man or politely kisses one at a New Year's party. He cannot help himself at that moment from acting enraged any more than he can pluck feathers from a telephone pole. Actually, most disturbances result from the second reason already discussed—ignorance. That is why I am writing this book. By eliminating ignorance I hope to reduce disturbances.

When you have reached step five ("you're bad for frustrating me") you are certain to feel angry. That doesn't mean, however, you will automatically hurt someone. Feeling as if you'd like to kill someone doesn't mean you would really kill someone. To do that you must go to the next step.

Step six: *"Bad people ought to be punished."*

In this step you have reached the point of no return. You will not rest now until you have inflicted pain on another person, not because it will necessarily do him some good, but because he is not good enough to deserve anything but pain, blame, and faultfinding.

This is the step that put people on the rack and stretched their bodies out of their sockets. This is the step that allowed torturers to pile heavy stones on top of people until the weight squished out their insides like grapes. This is the step that permitted medieval Europe to burn thousands of poor women for witchcraft. In short, *this is the most evil idea ever concocted by man.*

Not only is it false to believe that there are such things as bad people in the world, it is also wrong to believe that severe punishment helps them behave better. Since when is this supposed to be true?

The worst type of severe and harsh treatment is capital punishment. Do I have to argue the futility of expecting improved behavior from a decapitated man? Perhaps I have to argue against the futility of being harsh in other ways, however. Torture is perhaps the most severe pain a person can experience. Recently the American POW's came home from North Vietnam. Some of them were treated shamefully and brutally. They were tortured to punish them for flying bombers over North Vietnam, or to get them to make propaganda statements against the war. Their captors thought of them as bad people who deserved inhuman treatment. But as far as we can tell now, most of those prisoners did not regret fighting against North Vietnam, they did not make propaganda statements against the war, and they didn't feel one bit kindlier toward their captors because they were beaten for their behavior.

The same applies to you and the members of your family. When you are treated as though you are evil I can bet you last year's whips you do not want to be the soul of cooperation. When your wife gripes about your earning power and compares your hardest efforts to your more successful friend you can be certain you are not going to take her cutting remarks as a pep talk to go out and make a million for your "sweetheart."

When your husband keeps finding fault with you for not straightening up the house and points out how wasteful you are for not eating the heels of the bread, you normally do not want to go around with a smile on your face as you turn off unnecessary lights, pick up loose newspapers, and clean off lunch dishes. That kind of treatment takes the zip right out of you. You sense you are being punished and regarded as a bad person, and it doesn't do one bit of good for your soul. In fact, you almost invariably do worse because you're being blamed, and you practically always want to be mad and punishing in return.

If you think you can truly change bad behavior with violent methods, then get back to your history book. The few times it has worked it has required force of such magnitude that the behavior was changed only as long as the force hung over the victim's head. Once free of this threat, the victim did as he wanted.

When we face this matter realistically we will have to agree we can get more flies with honey than with vinegar. The worse someone is to you the nicer you ought to be to him. Only by making him feel foolish for being so ridiculously angry will he let up on his approach. Killing with kindness is much saner and more humane than killing with violence.

But does it work? You bet it does. Only a far-out screwball remains immune to smiles, politeness, and friendliness. If the person you must deal with is not plain crazy, you can be assured his behavior will improve greatly as you reverse the usual way of dealing with nasty treatment, that is, by being nicer and more caring.

Is Righteous Anger an Exception?

Most of you will agree that getting mad because you didn't get what you wanted is foolish if what you wanted is petty and insignificant. If you want to go swimming tomorrow and it rains, practically anyone in the world would say you were being a dunce and a bumpkin to get mad at the weather. Practically everyone would think you'd be an immature and very impulsive person if you smashed your dishes or furniture just to show another person how angry you were.

But what about those cases when you feel you have a serious reason to get angry? If you see a man beating a dog, don't you have the right to get furious with him and prevent the dog from being killed? Or if a bully is picking on your child, shouldn't you become furious and allow your righteous wrath to put him in his place?

As I see it, the answer is "No." When you come right down to it, *all* anger is righteous. In fact, anger wouldn't arise in the first place if you didn't think you were completely right in your opinion and that the other person was completely wrong. That even applies to things and nature. When you give your flat tire an angry kick you really are trying to tell the world that that tire had no right to go flat on you, that it has done a mean and dirty trick, and that it deserves a kick for being such a lousy tire.

In the final analysis a tire has as much right to go flat as a bully has to beat up on little kids. Something is wrong with both, and just because you or I dislike tires or bullies that behave that way we have no God-given right to insist they *can't* be that way. We do *not* have to have our own way, even when our desires are quite noble, or especially when we feel we are absolutely right. In all likelihood the other fellow thinks he's being completely right and proper, so who's to judge? And even if your frustrator cannot give a logical argument for his actions, he still does not have to behave as we would like because he has *the right to be wrong*.

This is the point most self-righteous people fail to see. They often correctly point to behaviors in others, such as prostitution, drugs, street crimes, or dropping out of school, and give good reasons why much of this behavior leads to real trouble and would better be avoided. But they also believe that just because they are so sensible, just because their own more mature experience convinces them of the evil of much of this behavior, and because they're certain persons would be happier following different paths, or that the whole world practically would agree with them, these people *must* stop their stupid ways.

Why must they stop being stupid, or stop acting like smart alecks? Why can't people act like fools if they really want to, and even if they know all the while they are being neurotic, self-defeating, and just plain dumb? What right do you or I have to insist that another person not smoke because he might get cancer? or that we have the right to forbid other people from becoming alcoholics, or thieves? Isn't that absurd, when you come right down to it? Don't people basically have the right to make wrong choices? And if they choose crime, too bad! They'll suffer for that eventually. But in the meantime, the right to make a dumb choice has to be granted them. You and I are not God and don't run the universe. So let's allow people to be what they will. If they hurt you or me, let's not get righteously angry over their dumb acts. Let's just arrest them and keep them out of society for a while or educate them to behave differently. And the way you can do that is by granting every person alive the right to be wrong. If you do this, you can never be righteously angry again.

Is Anger Ever Connected to Events from Your Childhood?

In other words, is anger always the result of a person's insisting on having his way? Isn't there ever a time when people are angry for unconscious reasons which started way back in childhood?

Of course there is. People can carry grudges for years, even unconscious ones. Maybe you're still sore at your mother because she preferred one of your brothers or sisters to you. Or perhaps you're still hateful to the kid who accidentally shot out your eye with his BB gun. Lots of frustrations originate in childhood and are still the indirect cause of much of our resentments and hostilities today, but only because we allow those events to upset us. Once again, the analysis of these past behaviors is really no different than is the analysis of behaviors and angers you encountered yesterday. You thought you wanted certain states and then you neurotically went ahead thinking you had to have what you first wanted. Childhood frustrations make you angry today because *today* you make the same demands you made years ago.

Gwenn was a real bombshell of a female. She tossed her curves around as well as a pitcher, but in her case she wasn't playing around, she was deadly earnest. Her hatred for men was intense and had been since her adolescent years, when her dad feared her dating habits would lead to promiscuity and he repeatedly told her she was going to become a tramp. Her hatred toward her father generalized to all men, whom she wanted to lead on and then frustrate. It was her cute way of getting back at the male species. The only trouble with her whole scheme was that it left her lonely and so alienated from men that she missed out on the wonderful romances men were willing to share with her. It was to help her lower her walls and allow herself to be loved that she sought counseling.

I started out by showing Gwenn that although her dad

misjudged her intentions he did have the neurotic right to do so. Perhaps he had sexual problems and should be pitied rather than hated. If she would forgive him without forgetting what he had done, she would spare herself that constantly bitter feeling she had in the presence of men. This would allow her to warm up to them and they to her. And then her deepest desires as a woman could be realized.

"But I've had this resentment toward men for ten years. Won't it take me years to undo it?" she asked with interest.

"It doesn't have to take any more than a few weeks or months if you will stop believing the stuff you've been telling yourself all these years. Your reason for holding off men today is not that your father accused you of fooling around ten years ago, but because yesterday afternoon, when that salesman came to your office, you once again told yourself the same thing you had said for years: 'All men are bad. I'm going to punish them. They'll never think cheaply of me again.'

"Because you said those thoughts yesterday, you lost out yesterday. Had you not had such thoughts and had you recognized the difference between the salesman's intentions and those of your father you would not have been the slightest bit angry. In fact, you would have been flattered."

She quarreled with me more about how a long-standing habit *had* to have an inevitable effect over her, but I refused to agree with her. During the following weeks she reexamined those attitudes carefully and decided I was right. Then it was that she mellowed and permitted several fellows to take her out, only this time she was responsive and pleased with their attentions.

Anger and Jealousy

Among the angriest people in the world are the jealous ones. Most people do not recognize, however, that the jealous person is also one of the most fear-filled persons in the world, who has a very severe case of inferiority feelings. To overcome this, he rates himself almost exclusively on the reactions others have to him. Should his friends and loved ones pay him much attention, he thinks he is a fine person. If, however, they pay attention to someone else, he panics because he fears the worst has happened—he has become nothing.

This is why it does not make sense for the jealous mate to complain about not being able to trust his spouse. In reality he cannot trust himself, that is, he constantly distrusts *what he thinks of himself,* not what his spouse thinks of him. If he had more feeling for himself, it wouldn't be nearly so important what others thought of him. He is actually demanding that others do for him what he cannot do for himself. He wants you and me to think well of him under all conditions, but he cannot do that in his own behalf.

Do not defend yourself against the charges of a jealous person. Ask him instead why he must have such constant love, why he doesn't amount to a worthwhile person even if his suspicions are true, and then remind him that all that love he demands is not going to come his way as long as he makes such a pest of himself. It takes a saint to love someone who hates himself and who makes himself quite hateable in the process of trying to be loved.

Here then are the psychological causes of anger. This chapter should be studied over and over again until you have the sequence of anger completely mastered. Some of you may find this rather easy, but others will no doubt encounter great difficulty. Regardless of how hard it appears to be at first, do not give up. You will get better and better at the task the more you do it. Try always to remember that the nature of the frustration itself is of secondary importance to the creation of your feelings. Your anger comes from your thinking, not from the thing you are thinking about. Doing something about the frustration should come second, after you have gotten hold of yourself emotionally. Then, once that has been achieved, you are in a position to deal with the frustration itself.

4

Don't Be a Catastrophizer

ONE OF THE VERY WORST TENDENCIES WE HAVE AS MOR-
tals is to make big things out of little things. We blow
situations way out of proportion, and then after creating
these monsters we get all scared over what we have created. That often leads to anger. It is, therefore, very important to realize what is and what is not a catastrophe,
and what you can do when you *do* have a very serious
situation on your hands.

The next time you get upset over positively anything
ask yourself as soon as possible thereafter, and prefer-
ably before you get upset, if you aren't really being only
annoyed rather than tortured; if what you are experienc-
ing isn't only a sad event rather than a tragic event; and
if you can't live through the frustration without its killing you. If you believe the former, then you will only
suffer from annoyances and disappointments. If you believe the latter, you will *think* you're suffering catastrophes, earth-shattering events, and deadly issues. But are
you? Or is it just that you are talking yourself into thinking you are facing the end of the world!

The distinction is important to make because it will
determine if you will react calmly or neurotically. Some
authorities, such as Dr. Albert Ellis, insist that no event

is ever catastrophic. Most people, however, are not likely to agree with this, so I want to emphasize other facts about unhappy events and frustrations. The first is that most events are not so serious as we usually think they are, and the second is that even if an event *is* very serious, we only make it worse by getting ourselves upset over it.

Frustrations Are *Not* Disturbances

The latest findings from psychology are clearly showing us that being frustrated and being disturbed are not one and the same. Until you understand this distinction, you will not see how unhappy events cannot, in and of themselves, make you angry.

A frustration is the condition of wanting something and not getting it, or not wanting something and having it forced on you. When you want to stay home and sleep but cannot because you must go to work, that is a frustration. When you have been pleasant to someone and they take you for granted, that is frustrating. In each case you wanted something and did not get it.

Years ago psychologists told us that being frustrated automatically led to hostility. They called this idea the frustration-aggression hypothesis. Here's one way they came to that conclusion. They put a number of children in a room filled with very fine toys. The dolls talked and wet; the dollhouse was large, the electric iron worked, and so on. After letting the children get used to these super toys, they were taken to the room next door which was partitioned off from the first room by a curtain. This room was filled with inferior toys. The dolls weren't as pretty, the dollhouse was crummy, and the iron didn't get hot. The experimenters pulled up the curtain and left a screen separating the children from the first room so they were unable to get back to the tempting toys. In other words, they were being frustrated because they wanted to play with the swell toys but couldn't. All the time they were playing with the inferior toys the psychologists took note of their behavior and found that the aggressive behavior took a sudden jump up when these kids were frustrated. So they concluded that frustration leads to aggression.

Actually they only demonstrated experimentally what we have known all along. In fact, we have been taught this by everyone we have ever come in contact with. Your parents taught you that being frustrated *must* lead to aggression and that the frustration actually caused the aggression.

What they forgot, however, was the fact that very often people are frustrated and do not become disturbed. How come? If frustration leads to disturbance, then why shouldn't it do so all the time? Now we can finally answer that question. Frustration never needs to lead to disturbance. That depends on us. If we think clearly when frustrated, we *can* avoid disturbance (anger, fear, depression). If we think neurotically when frustrated, we will feel disturbed.

In short, we have come to realize that a frustration and a disturbance are two entirely different states and that one does not *need* to follow the other, although it often does. All of you know some people who seem to have everything they could ever want and yet they complain all day long. I've known people who had successful professions, were well married, had their health, had lovely and obedient children, and still griped about lack of spending money, not being popular enough, or the weather. Others whom I've known have had to scrape for everything they had, were not in good health, hardly ever got out of the house, and almost never complained or seemed down in the mouth. How was this possible? Only by separating frustrations from disturbances. Can you now understand why you can be very frustrated and *not* disturbed, while others can be mildly frustrated and *very* disturbed?

Most Frustrations Are Quite Tolerable

If you have agreed with me this far and accept the idea that our frustrations do not cause our disturbances, you may still not want to concede that the two aren't related in some distant way at least. True, they are indirectly connected, because if you did not have a frustration you would not be disturbed, or at least you would not even need to talk yourself out of being disturbed. After all, a frustration requires of us a lot of work if we're going to take it calmly, and to that extent it is connected with our feelings. If, therefore, you can learn not to see so many events in your life as frustrations, or to see that the frustrations you do have aren't nearly so serious as you might allow yourself to think, you would clearly reduce the likelihood of your being disturbed.

To do this you have to think over your frustrations much more carefully than you have in the past. You have to understand what is really necessary in this world and what isn't. And what do psychology and medicine have to say about that? When you come right down to it, all we truly need in this world are food, shelter, clothing, and physical stimulation. Without any of those necessities you would die or lose your sanity. I'm not suggesting, of course, that we limit our lives just to those essentials merely because being loved isn't necessary, for example, or having a good job isn't crucial. Being loved and having good work are important but not necessary. It is frustrating not to be close to others or to be working on a boring job all day, to be sure. However, it would not be unbearable, as you might be inclined to think if either of these conditions suddenly entered your life.

You would not die if you were never loved dearly by someone. Only recently I received my umteenth emergency call from a bright lad who was eating his heart out because he broke up with his girl friend. I tried to get him to see that not being engaged any longer must certainly be regrettable and sad, but that was the only way that event was frustrating him. He in turn decided to make a serious disturbance over his being frustrated (not being loved), and had a deuce of a time accepting the fact that this frustration was hardly as bad as he was making it. Once he considered the possibility that being rejected is actually completely harmless, he cooled off nicely and went out looking for a new girl friend.

Millions of frustrations are far more easily tolerated than we usually think. Children's not finishing their dinners is not an awful frustration, just the waste of a few cents. And if a few cents bother you, put the plate in the refrigerator until later. A person swerving in front of you in traffic is not doing something that calls for a nuclear explosion. It isn't awful to have someone honking his horn impolitely behind you—it's only slightly annoying. Not getting your raise can hurt your pocketbook but not you, unless you let it. And that's the point, isn't it? Frustrations are not usually earthshaking to begin with—they can be tolerated quite nicely if we make the effort. Secondly, frustrations, even if they *are* severe, don't have to lead to disturbances unless we allow them to.

Why Distinguish Between Annoyances and Catastrophes?

If you think that what is happening to you is going to kill you, then you surely aren't going to sit still and let people run all over you. But if you do not think something is the end of the world, you're going to take it calmly and not get angry over it. Whether your emotions take one direction or the other will depend entirely on what happens at this point.

One man I counseled with told me how furious he was because his older brother wanted some support money from him to help take care of their mother. My client couldn't afford additional payments to his mother's welfare and in addition didn't think they were necessary since his mother had a trust fund which could have supported her easily. But it bothered him considerably to think his brother would try to squeeze a few extra dollars out of him for personal services in the care of their mother.

"But it is not right," Bill insisted. "I've been fair with Henry in every request he's ever made of me. But when he pulled this stunt I just felt he was taking me for a sucker."

"No, that's not why you're angry, Bill," I stated. "Nothing you've said so far sounds neurotic or unreasonable, and to become angry you've got to say angry things to yourself."

"Such as?"

"Such as, 'It's *awful* to be treated unfairly by my brother.'"

"How does that make me angry?"

"Because you make catastrophes out of annoyances. It

isn't true, for instance, that it really is awful to be treated unfairly by your brother. Prove to me it's terrible. How has it hurt you? Not how have you hurt yourself over it, but how has it hurt you? So he accuses you of being a miser. So what? Are you a miser? No? Then let him have his opinion and you can have yours.

"If on the other hand you were to have told yourself: 'Wow, what a screwball I have for a brother! He wants to squeeze blood out of a turnip when he knows very well I haven't got it, and worst of all it isn't even necessary to get more. Well, the old boy will just have to go to Mom's trust fund and support her with that money. Maybe that will leave less for him when she passes away, but I can't help that. I don't know what's come over the old boy, but he sure has gotten inconsiderate over the years. Hope he gets over it. However, if he doesn't, that's his problem, not mine.'

"Now, Bill, if you had spoken and thought to yourself in that vein, could you possibly have been upset?"

"I suppose not. By not making a big thing of his accusations I simply couldn't have reacted too emotionally in any way at all, could I? In other words, it would have been no different than his saying hello to me. If I'd make a big thing out of that, then I run the risk of being disturbed. If not, then I'm going to be undisturbed. Right?"

"Right."

Anger Can Cover Up Your Fear

Sometimes the angriest person, instead of being the most assured and confident, is actually the most scared. That's right—angry people are often covering up deep fears of inadequacy and fear of failure. Look at some typical human behavior to understand this. When a person is panicky, is he docile or furious? If four bullies back you in a corner, are you going to collapse in a heap or are you going to fight like a madman? Obviously you could do both, but the fact that you might easily fight like a wounded tiger proves my point. You'd fight with an unbelievable intensity simply because you were so very terrified.

In terms of human behavior taken from everyday life, the case of the jealous mate is perhaps the most illustrative. Betty is a very nice person who finally became acquainted with a fellow she liked. He had broken off with a girl friend before going with Betty, and she knew all about her. If the two of them would go out to a bar or restaurant and this other girl was also there, Betty became afraid her friend might be attracted to his former girl again. This brought out anger against her boyfriend, Eddie, whom she accused of deliberately bringing her to a place where he could meet his old girl friend.

The anger was meant to correct the possibility of her losing out in a romance to this other girl. Only by acting indignant did she think she was able to protect herself from the fear of losing her boyfriend.

Once in a lighthearted mood Eddie told Betty where he and his former friend had parked and necked. Thereafter she was all over him trying to find out how often he had been with her, what they did together, and whether he liked being with her, Betty, as much as he had enjoyed being with that other girl. All the while she put him through his daily third degree she was fully aware of the bad effect it was having on Eddie. It was becoming plain to her that she was becoming a great big, boring pain in the neck but she couldn't do anything about it. Even though she could see his affections slipping away from her, she had to bug him about his feelings for that girl, until he eventually broke off his romance with Betty and looked for someone else who didn't bother him all the time.

This example illustrates how her catastrophizing about being rejected literally brought on the rejection, and how the anger was a direct outgrowth of her intense fear. Had she not been so afraid of losing her lover she could never have been so bitter about the harmless events she ran into.

One of the saddest examples of how fear brings on anger is easily seen in the parent who cannot stand to be corrected. Should the child of one of these parents show Mom or Dad where he or she is mistaken, the parent becomes intensely defensive and angry at having his or her intelligence or sincerity questioned.

A high school boy questioned and disagreed with his father's statement about the relative harm of marijuana as against alcohol. In a few minutes the father was so incensed at having his authority questioned that he struck his boy so hard the boy was knocked against the wall and slid to the floor. Harsh words followed until the boy was ordered out of the house, although he had nowhere to go.

The father would have claimed he was teaching his fresh kid a lesson, and would hardly have understood that he made a catastrophe out of being disagreed with. Once he believed it was horrible and unbearable to have his son disagree with him, he became afraid of appearing wrong. This was so scary that he had to defend his image as an infallible father to the point where he became very fallible indeed. The fear of being wrong blinded him to the sensible realization that he certainly could be wrong, and that even if he weren't, it hardly mattered that his son disagreed with him. And finally he did not see the obvious fact that the son would not now politely agree with his father even if he could see that he was mistaken.

These defensive adults who always have to be right and who get all bothered at the prospect of being shown up are among the most unsure of all. They fear being mistaken so much that they become violent to avoid facing the truth. Angry people are often the most scared and the most inadequate. If they weren't so frightened, they'd hardly make so much of innocent events and get into blind rages over incidents a kid could overlook.

Do You Ever Have to Have Your Way?

I pointed out previously that all anger is technically righteous because you have to believe you're one hundred percent correct or you couldn't get riled up in the first place. Anger always says, "I don't deserve this kind of treatment, so therefore it must stop this instant." You can believe this about things or about people, it makes little difference. There is one difference, however, and that is that you become more incensed if you think the unfair treatment could have been avoided than if it was almost inevitable. For example, the tires of your car have gone thirty thousand miles and should be replaced. You haven't done that, however, and so you get a flat when you least want or can stand one. You'll tell yourself, "I wish I hadn't got a flat at this time." This is a sensible and healthy as well as a painless statement to make. Next you may foolishly tell yourself, "Therefore, I shouldn't have one because it is frustrating to have to fix a flat, especially when I'm in a rush to get to a party."

After a moment's reflection, however, you might decide that you really had that flat coming to you since you've already been pushing your luck what with having thirty thousand miles on those tires. Though you might be mightily frustrated over the inconvenience and even disgusted at yourself for being such a tightwad, you would probably get over this issue easily enough since you knew you deserved just what you got.

But suppose you were frustrated over something that you had nothing to do with, something completely undeserved, while those who were guilty and deserved punishment received praise. Don't you have the moral right and wouldn't it be healthy to be resentfully angry?

The answer is still "No." Take the case of Ruth. After ten years of marriage she and her husband were divorced and he remarried. Their nine-year-old son was granted to the custody of the father because Ruth allowed herself to become so disturbed the year before during a quarrel with her husband that she deserted the family and became pregnant. Before that she was very giving, bent over backward to please her partner, and made sacrifices in her career. Whenever he wanted her to help with mowing the lawn or polishing the car, she never hesitated to pitch in for the sake of the marriage and his happiness.

The hatred Ruth carried inside her was unbelievable. She dreamed of killing her husband. She was sick to the stomach much of the time. Her appetite was shot. Sleeping through a whole night was out of the question. And her patience with her newborn child was rapidly wearing thin. Was she righteously angry? You'd better believe it! In her opinion she didn't deserve a thing she got and she was additionally sore over the fact that her husband came out smelling like a rose when it was he who should have been doing all the suffering. Try counseling someone in this predicament sometime and you'll see why psychotherapists chew their pipe stems!

First I had to show her that there was no law against her getting the shaft. Secondly, it was truly not catastrophic if she did get treated unfairly while her husband was treated like royalty. Thirdly, he was not a wicked and evil person for conducting himself as he did; and fourthly, trying to kill him or punish him severely wasn't really helpful to her situation at all. I will pretend that you, the reader, are Ruth and that I am trying to debate these four points with her.

1. Ruth, the real reason for your being mad is that you don't think you should be frustrated, that you shouldn't have lost your child, that your lover should have married you, and that the courts should have punished your husband instead. Granted, you may be right about all those points, but why does that mean you must get what you want merely because you're right? Since when is this supposed to be a fair world? Who says we must be decent to others? Who says all people will be treated fairly and justly? This is an imperfect world and sometimes it stinks, so you'd better get used to the smell.

Sure, you wanted things to turn out in your favor, Ruth, and that's a healthy and sensible desire on your part. However, your anger arises not because you didn't get your way but because you foolishly thought you *had* to have your way. Who says so? Show me the law that states that Ruth Smith cannot get the shaft but everyone else in this silly world can? Your trouble is that you've confused wanting fair treatment with thinking you had to have fair treatment. *Why* do you have to have fair treatment? Sure, it would be better if you got it, but so would it be better if we never had floods, cancer, war, and bad breath. That hardly means that I've a right to insist I get all these desires fulfilled merely because

72

they are important to me, does it?

2. The fact that your husband has beaten you in this affair and you've been abused is not the end of the world as you keep thinking it is. How is it the end of everything? Why should you go out and shoot someone over it? If you shoot your husband, you'll go to jail for the rest of your life, your son won't have either of his natural parents to live with then, and neither will your new baby. Talk about a catastrophe, what do you think you'd have then? Surely you don't want to make things *worse*, do you?

Also, since the boy is already nine years old, you need to wait only another five years or so and he'll be in a position to pick the parent he wants to live with. Can't you wait five years? And what about the possibility of your husband's dying tomorrow or the next day? That would get you your son back immediately, wouldn't it? And lastly, even though he fooled everyone this time, it's highly unlikely that he can continue doing this forever. Give him enough rope and he'll show his true colors and hang himself. Then the courts may declare him unfit as a father, his wife might leave him, or the boy might become so upset under his care that you could turn the matter over to a state agency and have the boy removed for his protection. In short, Ruth, the game is hardly over yet. We can't tell what the future has in store for any of us, so cool it and wait and see. This is not the end of the world. It may in fact be the beginning of many very good things. You say I'm wrong? How do you know I'm wrong? Can you foretell the future? If so, put your coat on and let me take you to the races this afternoon and we'll make a bundle on your predictions. So how can you be so sure the future is going to be so bleak? It may be, of course. But it just as easily might not be. So I insist this whole thing is not terrible or catastrophic.

3. One of the reasons you are so burned up over this situation is that you believe your husband is wicked and evil. That's strange for you to say, since you've been confessing some of the most evil thoughts to me that I've heard since the Marquis de Sade strangled his last mistress. If your husband is evil, so are you. In fact, you'd be more evil than he because he hasn't wanted to roast you over a spit as you have him, he hasn't even suggested he wanted you dead, and he isn't losing any sleep over all the gruesome ways he can torture you. But you are. And still you don't think of yourself as being wicked, only mistreated. Well, who's to say he doesn't also feel abused by the things you did during the marriage?

Even if I were to agree with you that he has treated you wickedly, I would still have to ask why a decent person like your husband would do something so evil? There would have to be a good reason for it. If you separated his behavior from himself, you could then disapprove and hate his behavior without hating him as a human being. And what reasons would he have for mistreating you this way? As I told you once before, it would have to be because he was either stupid, ignorant, or disturbed. Now we know he's not stupid because he isn't mentally retarded. In fact, he's rather bright. So is he ignorant? Possibly. But I don't think so. He knows what he's doing—in fact he's pretty shrewd about the whole thing. So we can't excuse him on the ground that he didn't realize you'd be upset having your son taken away. Then he'd have to be disturbed, wouldn't he, to treat you so badly? He too must think people are bad and should be treated severely, just as you think. Millions of people punish others for behavior which isn't nearly so bad as the punishment they feel justified in giving.

Since he has this neurotic belief about the need to punish people, how can we blame him for doing what he was trained to believe? He is quite sincere when he thinks you're bad and shouldn't be around this boy. That's stupid, perhaps, but you can't convince him of that. Therefore, he must act according to what he believes. He really can't do otherwise, can he? We could be sympathetic toward him for being so disturbed that he would actually hate you when he once loved you dearly and had a child by you.

4. If you give him a bad time, what will it accomplish? Kill him and, as I've already said, you practically orphan your child and put yourself in jail for most of your life. You've got to be just plain stupid to solve your problems that way. However, let's say you don't kill him but just want to make life miserable for him. What then? Will he change? Will that get your child back? And if you upset him sufficiently to make him truly suffer, what will that do to your son? Is it good for the boy to have a father around him who is losing his marbles? Will torturing him get him to feel sorry for you and to regret how he treated you? How so? Won't he in fact be inclined to hate you even more and possibly try to take away your second child? That's not unlikely, you know, because people always get more bitter and hateful when you treat them hatefully. Anger begets anger, Ruth. No, I'm afraid you'll have to rethink this whole thing or it will eat you alive. In fact, it's doing a good job of that already. Your anger is hurting you much more than it is hurting him. Wasn't it bad enough that you lost your marriage, your child, and your lover without also losing your health, your san-

ity, and your large intestine?

I will leave Ruth at this point with all her miseries and remind you that you do not need to have your way even if you mightily deserve it. Be careful how you treat this matter, for it can kill you if mishandled.

Dictators Are Catastrophizers

The one type of person most people do not want to be close to is a dictator, someone telling them to do this or that without any regard to their own wishes. Has it ever occurred to you, however, that when you're angry you are *always* a dictator? It's easy enough to see this when you recall what it is that makes you sore in the first place: your demands. And what is a dictator but a walking demand? Isn't that what bugs us about them? Don't we dislike their ordering us around without regard to our desires, having consideration only for their desires? Think it over carefully and you'll see that dictators are hated because they want to hurt others who don't give them their way. They think people who disobey them are bad and should be severely punished, and that being frustrated is the end of the world.

What has this to do with you? How do Mussolini, Hitler, and Stalin relate to you? Simply this: When you get angry, resentful, bitter, or hateful you are no different than these big-league dictators. The fact that you're little-league stuff doesn't change the basic fact at all that you think everything should run as you say or else you'd be dealing with a catastrophe.

This point is easy to understand if you're talking about a sadist whipping his girl friend into submission. And we can see how a man is a dictator when he's an army sergeant and runs his rookies ragged. What he says goes, and he doesn't think over very carefully what he says. But what about the devoted mother who is trying to get her child to study and make good grades? Or what about the father who gets mad at his son for calling his mother a witch? Are these people being dictators just because they're getting angry? Certainly they are!

The mother who is trying to make her child earn good grades isn't a dictator for trying. It is when she makes a mountain out of a molehill and *insists* the child will earn good grades: that's the stuff dictators are made of. They demand their own way and believe that those who disobey them are bad, should be severely dealt with, and that mistakes are horrible!

If the mother could look at this problem more sanely, she'd realize (*a*) it would be very fine indeed if her daughter were to become a topnotch student; (*b*) about the only way she will gain that end is to study much harder than she has; (*c*) therefore she, the mother, had better stimulate the girl toward studying harder and if necessary penalize her for goofing off; and (*d*) if penalizing her doesn't work she should not feel the girl is bad but accept calmly what she can't change.

Were she to do this, her daughter would not become spiteful and use poor grades as a way of punishing her Hitler-like mother.

However, if the mother takes the other road—that of the dictator—she will follow the irrational process: (*a*) getting poor grades is unbearable; (*b*) she will have to make the girl work harder to get top grades; (*c*) if the girl does not produce, scold her, slap her, let her know how bad she is for defying her mother, and insist angrily that she must do as her mother says; and finally (*d*) keep this up until the girl sees how right her mother is and gives in.

It doesn't take a genius to see how the second procedure will not succeed. Yet millions of well-meaning parents turn into dictators every day in the belief that their children have to do what's good for them because the parents think they're facing a life-and-death issue and are therefore right. This simply doesn't make any difference, however. Being right does not mean you have the God-given right to insist the other person must change his ways or agree with you. If I tell you two plus two are five, you have the moral right to think I'm nuts and to try to change my mind. But you do not have the moral right to force me to think two plus two are four. I still have the right to be wrong, regardless of what you think. To behave otherwise is to violate the sanctity of my brain. You have no business forcing your thoughts on me. How would you like it if I didn't like the ideas you had floating around in your head and insisted you stop having those thoughts? Wouldn't you think that rather absurd and even cruel of me? And suppose, further, that I could actually reach inside your head with a tool and alter your thinking so that it conformed with what I regarded as proper and correct. You'd have to admit anyone who would control the thoughts of others is certainly a dictator.

Well, then, put yourself in your proper place when you get angry with others. Your anger signifies that you don't like another person's actions and therefore his thoughts, and intend to control both from now on against that person's will. That's why you must use force in the first place. If you didn't need force to get others to see your point of view, you wouldn't be angry, would you? And is this not what a dictator relies on? He has the moral right to disapprove of your views, but does he have the moral right to force you to deny your views?

No, obviously not, although he has the neurotic right. By this I mean he has the right to be wrong merely because he is human and imperfect. That's why you can protect yourself from becoming a dictator against someone who is acting like a dictator against you. If you forgive him the disturbances that make him what he is and allow him the neurotic right to think he should run the world, and if you do not dictatorially insist he cannot go around thinking you can't think two and two are five, you then spare yourself the same silly stuff you protest in him.

In the final analysis it is my getting angry because you are unreasonable that turns me into a dictator over your being a dictator.

Then how in the world is one supposed to deal with people who neurotically go around insisting I can't believe my government is wrong, that capital punishment is morally evil, or that the white race is superior, that only churchgoers are decent folk, or that we ought to distribute the wealth and become communistic?

We deal with them very simply. Allow them to think what they will even though you may think they're wrong and you're right. They have a right to their views, just as you have a right to yours. To insist they cannot believe as they do is simply childish on your part, even if you are defending your country. You don't run the world, and if you don't like the views of others, change them through example and debate, not force.

This may still not prove satisfying to you, so let's look at the example of the father who became incensed because his son called his mother a "witch."

From what I have been saying above you will by now predict that the father would better say to himself that his son has the right to be wrong and to think his mother is a witch if that's what he truly believes. For the father to insist his son cannot think this way makes an immoral dictator out of the father. Which is worse, an immoral dictator or a sincere son who dislikes his mother?

"So you're suggesting the father should keep his mouth shut and let his son say anything he wants to his mother. Is that it?" you are probably asking.

My answer is, "Of course not." Since when would any sensible father sit back and let his son grow up so disrespectful of his parents? He'd have to be cowardly or very neurotic in other ways to tolerate such nonsense. The point I wish to make, however, is that the father need not get mad to control the boy, he could merely be assertive. It's a choice of his being aggressive in order to be assertive as contrasted with merely being assertive. Must you, for instance, always be mad to be firm? Couldn't you stand your ground without boiling up inside? Why not? Who says we must automatically get mad if we want to get tough? Couldn't the father tell the son in a quiet way to apologize to his mother? He could do this if he reasoned that it was not the end of the world if his wife was called a bad name, and that his fine boy wouldn't say something like that unless he were terribly upset, in which case anyone could be excused for making an occasional unkind remark. The father has probably made dozens just like it in his lifetime.

Suppose the son will not apologize. Then couldn't both parents refuse to speak with him further until he asked for forgiveness? By ignoring him until he has regained his senses they might correct the matter harmlessly.

What if the boy still insisted on swearing at his mother? What then? Well, if he were old enough he could be asked to live elsewhere until he learned to treat her with the decency he would give a stranger. And if he would not go? They then could simply let him be and not trouble themselves over his rude manners. Must they storm endlessly about a situation they can't change? That's what Martha thought when her stepson would not leave her house. She wanted him out because he was a bully, he intimidated his father, spoke most disrespectfully to her, and even gave her children from a prior marriage a whale of a bad time. When Martha asked for assistance against his tyranny the father was too scared himself to take on the tall, husky bully. So the nineteen-year-old kid had his way. At first Martha cried a lot. Then she got angrier and angrier that she couldn't do what she wanted to in her own house. He had taken over and had his way and there wasn't a thing she could do about it. Finally, after some counseling, she learned to put up with his rudeness by accepting it philosophically. The only way she ended the problem was to wait patiently for the months to roll around until the rascal married and left for good.

Martha had acted like a dictator for years while that boy was growing up. She kept on insisting he shouldn't do this or that. But that only made the fellow more angry. You see, he was a dictator too and insisted on getting his way. In this case, he was the stronger of the two dictators, so he won out. But, righteous or not, Martha was insisting neurotically that he had no right to act as he was acting and had to stop it. It wasn't until she accepted the fact that he *could* tyrannize the family, that he could drop cigarette ashes on her clean floor, drop his clothes wherever he wanted, leave his room in a shambles, etc., that she calmed down. By not being dictatorial about it she calmly did what little she could and waited in relative peace until he left.

No matter how just one is, to get angry for any cause requires that you become a dictator, that you get your way, and that others cannot have their way. This needn't concern you if you are protecting others or yourself, even though to do so would make you a dictator. For example, had Martha's stepson physically attacked her, I would have hoped she could protect herself but keep her wits and escape harm, or even take some punishment if that was inevitable without going into a dangerous frenzy. This may be too much to expect from a mere mortal, however, and one could completely understand her furiously defending herself, kicking him, scratching his face, and even brandishing a knife in self-defense. At such a critical time, being unneurotically angry would be desirable but not so important as being efficient in one's self-defense regardless of how it was accomplished.

Self-pity and Anger

Have you ever observed how often depression and anger seem to go together? Self-pity is one of the three ways people depress themselves, self-blame and other-pity being the other two. When you pity yourself you first have to make a mountain out of a molehill and, as I've already tried to show, making catastrophes can lead to anger. But when you pity yourself instead of scaring yourself, you build up the injustice so much that soon you've got yourself talked into thinking the most awful things have happened to you and someone ought to be badly punished for causing these bad things.

The self-pitier is his own enemy much more than he can possibly imagine. He doesn't want to make waves with those around him, so he gives in and lets others have their way while denying himself even the slightest amount of satisfaction. This silly arrangement can go on for days, weeks, months, and yes, even years. The person who is being given into usually feels fine, but the self-pitier becomes more and more bitter until one day all hell breaks loose. Dorothy was a good case in point.

During the seventeen years of her marriage she never had one good, assertive blowup with her husband. Oh, there was plenty she didn't like about his behavior, you can be sure, but she never said much. When she talked to him about his endless Saturdays on the golf course and all those fishing vacations he took rather than keeping her company tending to the yard on weekends or taking a shopping vacation to Chicago, she said it in such a passive manner he never got the message. She would then get into a depressed mood and brood bitterly. The first ten years were filled with the tears of self-pity while hubby went off with the boys, had his beers, his bowling, and other masculine pleasures. The next five years were filled with indifference. She became cold toward him sexually and no longer had the will to have climaxes. Eventually she could hardly tolerate his touching her. She was hurt badly and was slowly beginning to turn her self-pity into bitterness. It finally came in the form of a legal announcement that practically knocked her husband off his feet. Whereas one day he was the life of the party, the next day he was a quivering bowl of jelly visibly shaken, very contrite, and not a little bewildered by the impending divorce.

The little blossom showed her thorns. It took seventeen years for her to rear up on her hind legs because she had the bad habit all those years of making a catastrophe out of standing up to him and really letting him know how deeply she was frustrated. She thought being rejected was awful and unbearable, so she tolerated all for the sake of being accepted. But when her feelings got so intense she sensibly decided she could live without his love, and in fact wouldn't have accepted it then even when he offered it with no strings attached. Can you imagine how angry and bitter you've got to be to do that?

People, beware of the self-pitier! Though he may seem easy to get along with for years, the day of reckoning is around the corner. That fearful and long-suffering, passive, imitation of a human being can yet develop resentment that you wouldn't believe. When that happens a relationship is practically over. In twenty years of marital counseling I have known very few marriages that were patched up when self-pity turned into bitterness. It made no difference whether the other mate threatened violence, suicide, became depressed, or pleaded on hands and knees. Once that point of bitterness was reached there was usually no turning back.

No matter how you look at it, catastrophizing is a very bad psychological habit. It is the equivalent of instant neurosis. It can make you nervous, anxious, chronically worried, or depressed. But these neurotic states can in their turn lead often to anger, bitterness, and resentment so great forgiveness is all but impossible. It behooves you, therefore, if you would learn to control your anger, to control your tendency to make mountains out of molehills. Remember always that most of the frustrations from which you suffer are really not all that awful, and the few that are bad can be handled with much more calm and acceptance than you generally think possible. The rest of this book will attempt to show you how this can be done.

5

Watch That Blame!

BLAME IS THE CENTRAL ISSUE OF ANGER. WITHOUT blame hate, cruelty, and needless pain of all kinds would be unthinkable. It is therefore very important to control and diminish blame as much as possible in our everyday behavior and to understand precisely what I mean by blame.

Blame occurs when you find fault with someone's behavior *and* with that person at the same time. If you think people are bad because they frequently do bad things, then you are a blamer and are doing one of the most neurotic, dangerous, and unprofitable acts people can commit.

Instead of blaming people for their actions, it is infinitely wiser and more charitable (as well as efficient) to separate their behavior from their selves. You do this all the time with your children, I hope. Your child spills his milk and you dislike the mess. But do you also hate your child? Do you think he's bad because he did something bad? If you do, you're a blamer and I can predict you will have a tense household. If the home is calm although you do blame, then figure the tension has gone underground and everyone is afraid to say anything lest you get mad and hit the ceiling. However, you'll see that disturbance come to the surface at some later date. Therefore, make every effort to separate the person from his behavior and the sinner from his sins. Then become concerned with correcting a mistake maker rather than putting him down.

Suppose you hang a picture on the wall with a small nail and the picture falls to the floor a few hours later. Would you blame the picture because it was too heavy for the nail and insist it was an evil picture? Or would you blame the nail for not being more stout and capable of holding a heavier picture? Neither, I hope, or you'd be more neurotic than you already suspect you are. What I hope you would do is forget about blaming the picture or the nail and decide what you have to do about the problem. Either get a lighter picture or a heavier nail. That's being *problem*-oriented, not *blame*-oriented. But notice, it is also being *fault*-oriented. If you don't know what's at fault, you can't very well change the trouble. So being fault-oriented is good and not at all the same as blame-oriented. In the latter case you'd think the picture was sinful and so you'd step on it because it fell, and in the case of fault you'd decide what had to be done because you now knew what was wrong and this knowledge would lead you to a solution.

This takes us to the next question most people ask at this point. "If I don't blame him, whom should I blame?" The answer is, never blame anyone. Remember, blame means you are damning some thing or person and that is not justified or efficient. It's not justified because you cannot prove a thing is bad because it did you harm, and the more you blame someone the worse he gets, not better.

Blame Is Never Justified

If I run my car into yours, you are not morally correct to blame me for the accident. I grant you I was responsible for the accident, but I am not blameworthy because of it. How so? Because responsibility and blame are not the same. When you debate with me and suggest the accident was my fault, you are trying to place reponsibility for the action. When you get angry at me you are trying to convince me I am a damnable person, a good-for-nothing who can never drive well again because I was responsible for this accident. I'll be damned if I agree with that last statement!

The accident has only proved one thing as far as I can see: I am not a superduper driver. It proves nothing about me as a person. As a person I am as important to myself as you are to yourself. Our worth to each other never changes despite how much our value changes toward other people. If I am a poor driver, I won't have much value to those who value good driving, such as race drivers, insurance companies, the police, and hot-rodders. But since when does that mean I must devalue myself just because I have no value to those groups?

When you feel you are no good because you have no aptitude for earning a living, being a decent mother, student, or citizen, do not allow those weaknesses and deficiencies to interfere with the full right you have to honor yourself as a person with the capacity to enjoy life.

Unless you make this distinction you are damning some of the nicest people in the world. For example, if your mother doesn't drive at the Monte Carlo races, she's no good. If your father isn't as smart as some of your teachers, he's worthless. And if your mate gets drunk at your birthday party, he or she should be completely rejected. That's what the blamer means whether he knows it or not.

To avoid this error, always separate the person from his actions. Criticize his actions if you find them faulty, but never attack the person, because perhaps he cannot help the fault you're criticizing. We were all made with different strengths and talents, and if being able to drive well or study efficiently or respect one's mate is not one of them, accept that and work around it if you can. But don't get angry at faults the person himself wishes he didn't have. That doesn't change them, and it often makes the behavior worse.

At this point my previous discussion of the reasons for people acting badly becomes relevant. I pointed out that people behave badly for three very good reasons: stupidity, ignorance, and disturbance. If you see all objectionable behavior as a natural result of one of these three conditions (or combinations thereof), you surely cannot get very angry. This means we have the perfect and proper right to forgive anyone any kind of miserable and improper action. It is possible to forgive Hitler for killing millions of people, because he must have been pretty insane to feed people into gas furnaces. You can forgive the North Vietnamese soldiers for brutally torturing our POW's because that's their mentality for you. Some people are raised to believe torture is simply the thing to do to criminals. They're the criminals also, of course, because what they do is no better than what they claim their captives did. However, they don't believe that argument. They were taught differently, so we must expect them to behave differently.

Forgive but Never Forget

Are you now wondering what you're supposed to do if you're not to blame them? Should you throw up your hands when someone does you wrong and forgive him because he may be nutty and let it go at that? No, absolutely not. The trick is to *forgive everything,* and *forget nothing.*

By forgiving your enemy you avoid getting ulcers, while by not forgetting what he did you can study the problem and avoid trouble in the future. Roger was a very decent fellow who loaned his car and money liberally to his friends. But they did not treat him with the same courtesy, and he took this so badly he would bottle up his anger to the point where he became tense and occasionally snapped at people.

"Why do people abuse my good nature?" he complained.

"Because they're ignorant and disturbed and therefore should sometimes take advantage of nice guys like you," I responded.

"They *should* take advantage of me, you say? No, they shouldn't take advantage of a friend. That's the way I was raised to think."

"And it would be *better* if they didn't abuse a friend. But why must they do as you'd like merely because it's the decent thing to do? Must people be decent because you say so?"

"No, of course not. What do you suggest?"

"Forgive them so you don't remain angry another day. Do yourself a favor since they surely haven't done you any lately."

"Do myself a favor by forgiving them?"

"Yes. That protects you from getting mad, upset, resentful, and bitter. Wouldn't you enjoy being rid of those neurotic feelings?"

"That's why I'm here talking to you today."

"Then forgive them all their lousy behavior and you'll calm down nicely and quickly. Then do something positive about it."

"Like what?"

"Learn from your experience. Never forget who drove your car all over town and used up your gas and wasn't considerate enough to fill up the tank. And then never loan him the car again. That's what I mean by forgiving but not forgetting.

"By doing that, you would be changing the problem and not letting it happen again, while at the same time you wouldn't be fuming over it and hurting yourself, would you?"

Roger got the message very nicely. He learned to accept people's selfishness as a fact of life, but once he saw it he learned to avoid it. As he said to me later: "It's the same as with a tornado. I must learn what a tornado does and not blame the thing for being what it is. But I can usually do something about avoiding it and not letting it hurt me."

Forgiving others also means that you must be strong and healthy. Forgiveness is simply impossible in the weak and defensive. It is one of the most beautiful traits to develop, provided you back it up by not forgetting what happened to you. Should you forgive and forget what others unjustly did to you, then you're simply asking for another kick in the pants. In that case forgiveness indicates stupidity and weakness on your part.

The degree to which you can forgive others but not give in to their weaknesses in the future is an excellent measure of just how mature you are. Look around you

90

and examine the people in your life and see what the mature ones are really like. Aren't they decent and forgiving, and aren't they strong enough to say no after they've been taken advantage of?

Forgiveness also lets others grow and develop. Instead of putting people down, making them feel guilty, inferior, and defensive, forgiveness treats them kindly, assures them you still feel they have value as human beings and that they can overcome their errors. Whereas blame is one of the worst of human behaviors, forgiveness is one of the finest. It is the cornerstone of all the major religions in the world, and for good reason. Love and kindness are nothing if not a big dose of forgiveness. The person who forgives others cannot truly ever be angry and hateful.

The More You Blame Others, the Worse They Get

The single most important reason for forgiving others for behaving badly is to avoid teaching people to hate themselves. The less hate in the world the better. Therefore, the less blame you give to others the less blame they give themselves. This is especially true of the uneducated, the immature, and children. And to some extent it is true of us all.

If someone keeps on telling you how bad you are, you can bet your last bottle of poison that you're going to believe him after a while. Once this happens you take over where mother, father, or spouse left off and call yourself the same negative things they once called you. In fact, the people who originally accused you of being worthless can die and you'll still keep on calling yourself lousy things for the next fifty years, if you aren't careful. Hating yourself secretly, doubting your personal value, thinking everyone else is better than you makes you go through life with your psychological tail between your legs. And do you know why? Because you think you stink so badly no one would want to do anything with you. You find yourself friendless. Others are really not shying away from you. It is you who are shying away from others because you remember what a good-for-nothing you are and how nobody in his right mind could really want your company. In fact, this can get so bad you not only think others wouldn't want anything to do with you, you also become convinced others wouldn't want anything to do with your children. You attempt to convince your kids not to socialize with certain well-known segments of society or people of higher social and economic levels because you're positive your children will get rejected and they have no business being around people "better" than they are.

How sad! The faults of the parents are visited upon the children. I once counseled a young fellow who was doing well in school, was a handsome lad, and felt quite comfortable talking to his professors and to girls from all levels of society. Invariably, when he would proudly tell his parents he had had lunch with his department chairman or had taken Ms. Riches to a school dance they ridiculed him in the most sarcastic way imaginable.

"Who do you think you are, Tom? Don't you know those people are only being charitable to you? What the devil do you think they want to spend time with you for? They're using you and making fun of you behind their backs. Leave them alone. I told you and told you not to go to school. Stay with your own kind, son. You belong with our kind of people, not those snooty ones." And so it went. At times Tom became so unsure of himself that he kept his own company and was almost ready to leave school. At other times he would get infuriated with his parents for reminding him of his humble background and wanting to keep him among the uneducated and unsuccessful. In counseling I reminded Tom how well-meaning his parents were but how neurotic they were also.

"Your parents can't help what they're doing. They honestly believe you should not aspire to raise yourself in life. They believe they're both so worthless that they couldn't possibly have a worthwhile child. They are so convinced others will reject them that you must suffer from the same fate. You're their child so you can't be any better than they are.

"I've already explained to you how they got that way. Their parents blamed them for their errors. They were told about seven million times while they were growing up that they were no good, that they were stupid, that they were going to end up like jerks, that they ought to feel guilty over every mistake they made, and that every mistake they made only proved again how worthless they were. Now they've brainwashed you also into believing this nonsense. Fortunately you came to counseling before they could completely defeat you. If you examine closely all the junk they're trying to get you to swallow, I'm sure you can see how sincere they want to be but also how absolutely nutty they are."

I have never met anyone who was blamed a great deal who also thought he was a fine person. It is the shortest way to a beautiful inferiority complex. It is also the surest way to failure. And isn't that an interesting twist —those who are blamed the most for failing, eventually do the most failing. And why not? If you keep drilling into someone's head how good-for-nothing he is, how do you expect that person to have the confidence to do well? This inescapable fact should be clear to everyone: the more you blame people, the worse they get. Beat up your child for earning poor grades and his grades will go down, not up. If by some miracle they do go up, his self-esteem may not. If his self-esteem does not go down, his love for you will. Something must give. Frankly, when blame does work, the price is simply too great and is not worth it.

Another consequence that comes from blaming others is that they become much more hostile and angry with you. One of the best ways to get into a fight is to tell others how badly they do something, such as play bridge, and also intimate how disgusting they are because they play badly. The natural human tendency is to defend oneself when attacked. Where would this be more appropriate than with someone attacking your intrinsic worthwhileness?

This is all the more interesting because the blame in the first place is meant to correct someone's fault, not increase it. But the person being attacked is barely able to listen to what is being said about his behavior—all he hears is what is being said about him as a person. That's why blame often has such little effect on those who need correction. Our penal systems are an excellent case in point. How often does a man go to jail and get the feeling that the court, the police, and the prison guards are there to honestly help him? He's there to be punished, not corrected. He's there to suffer because society thinks he's bad and must be severely dealt with. And society apparently thinks the more he suffers the better a person he will be. This is arrant nonsense of the worst sort.

When you treat people as if they're trash, they more often than not behave like trash. When prisoners are treated like animals, they behave like animals. The problem is not the prisoners, it is in the way we treat them. We are only reaping what we sow. If we could stop blaming them and thinking they're bad, they would return our attitude with better behavior, not worse behavior. The reason for this is the fact that they would be free to pay attention to their behavior, not to what we think of them as persons.

Self-fulfilling Prophecies

The behavior you get from others is so closely determined by what you expect from them that you can actually predict what a person will do by what you expect from him. This was shown beautifully in an experiment with a group of schoolchildren. All these children were tested for several academic skills and intellectual levels. From this large group they sorted out all those children who were of approximately equal I.Q. and who could read, spell, and do math at about the same level.

This group was then divided into two, group A and group B. Group A was then turned over to a teacher and told: "These children are the cream of the crop. They're bright, capable, and eager to learn. Push them if you like because they can take it." The second group was turned over to a different teacher and told, "Sorry to have to do this to you, but you've got the slowest of the school. These kids have always had trouble learning and no doubt you'll soon see how tough it's going to be for them. However, try your best, but don't get discouraged if you don't see fabulous results."

After each teacher had worked with his group for a period of time, each teaching the same subjects, the students were retested. What were the results? Do I have to tell you? In case you're in doubt: group A learned much more than did group B. The prophecy had been fulfilled. One teacher thought his students could do well so they were treated like capable children and proved it. The other teacher thought he had dopes and somehow convinced them of this. And that's what he got, poor students.

You might protest that such results are only too obvious, that anyone knows what to expect under those conditions because they were even obvious to the children. You might insist none of that could happen if the instructor had less control over his subjects. This isn't true either, unfortunately. It makes no difference whether the subjects know they're being brainwashed or not. To prove this, the psychologists who did this study took a large group of rats and timed them all to see how fast they could learn to run a maze. Those rats who had approximately the same speeds were placed in the study groups. Again this group was divided into groups A and B and again the experimenters were told one group was quick, alert, and bright while the other was a pack of laggards, dullards, and experimental nincompoops. Each experimenter was urged to teach the rats certain skills and to test them after a specified period of time.

Do you think it would be possible for group A to know that its experimenter thought they were bright? and that group B knew its experimenter thought of them as stupid? How could such attitudes be communicated? After all, the experimenter is standing over the mazes, watches his stopwatch, makes his notations, and puts the rats back into their cages. How in the world could a person give some rats under those conditions a feeling of being superior or inferior? No one really knows. But we do know it can be done. Group A rats learned faster and faster while group B rats learned slower and slower.

Can you now begin to see what blame does? Can you see why so many men coming out of our prisons act worse than they did before imprisonment? If the guards, the police, and the courts take the attitude prisoners belong to the B group, then we've got to be releasing men who think they're bad, who need rough treatment to control them, and who may never learn to conduct themselves peacefully.

And can you see how this would influence you in your family life? The more you blame your children or spouse the worse that person is going to get. I hope that is apparent by now.

What's Good for the Goose Is Good for the Gander

Another feature about blame that escapes most of you is the fact that it is monstrously unfair because you end up being guilty of an injustice in the same way the person you are blaming is guilty. That is, you are no less guilty for punishing others with blame than they were for doing the act for which you are blaming them. For instance, we have been putting murderers to death for years under the following reasoning: (1) murderers frustrate us (true); (2) that makes them bad (false); and (3) therefore they had better be severely punished (false).

However, if *they* deserve death because of a bad act, then why shouldn't we kill the executioners of the murderers? After all, (1) the murderer too was frustrated (true); (2) he felt his frustrater was bad (false); and (3) therefore he should be severely punished (false).

97

Voilà, a murder! The murderer uses the same logic the state does, but because he doesn't have an army of policemen to track down the criminal he gets punished. Might makes right. One would think that what is good for the goose is good for the gander. Justice is clearly not involved here, only majority opinion. To treat him fairly the state would have to do something better to the murderer than the murderer did to his victim. To do the same makes the state as guilty as the man it is executing.

The same is obviously true on the personal level. Peter felt pressured by Jenny to visit her folks over the holidays. He hated the last trip more than most of the previous ones, and told her so. But in addition he felt so mad over her constant urging that he go where he didn't want to be that he decided to punish her for her thoughtlessness. So he immediately lost interest in sex. This frustrated her because she was made for making love and felt irritable when deprived of her sexual experience. Then he gradually stopped talking to her—another mortal blow; and he kept this up not for a few days, not for a few weeks, but for almost two months. During that time he didn't utter one single, solitary word to her for any reason. What he would have done if the house had caught fire escapes me!

No doubt Peter thought he was being quite justified. His wife had done him wrong, he would do her wrong. But where is the fairness? Isn't he the one who thought he was being treated unfairly, and isn't he the one who thought being treated unfairly was not right and decent? Then how could he justify being spiteful against Jenny when he was getting back at her in the same way she got to him?

Had he wanted to be free of her type of behavior (since he thought she was so completely wrong), he could have talked to her nicely and simply warned her that henceforth she would have to go visit her folks alone. If he had done that, he surely would have behaved more considerately than she. Again, what's morally right for me has to be morally right for you too.

A final example might make this point crystal clear. When your kids are yelling and you yell at them to stop, you are both in the same boat. You and they deserve the same treatment. If you think they deserve a spanking, then give yourself one also. Fortunately, however, an eye for an eye has long been recognized as an evil philosophy.

What Blame Does to You

The worst result of blaming others is the subject of this book. It is the anger that *you* must then carry around inside your body. This is far and away the most pointless personal effect blaming others has. As though it weren't bad enough that someone has done you wrong, you then swing into high gear and do to yourself what you wouldn't allow anyone else to do to you in a million years.

Let's take the case of revenge and hate. These twin emotions have caused some people an enormous amount of suffering which was far in excess of the suffering they received at the hands of others.

Terry was a young father who was sent to me by the court. He had already been arrested for speeding, driving while intoxicated, and forceful entry into the home of his former in-laws. They were caring for his young daughter, and they and his ex-wife refused (unfairly and without court consent) to allow him to visit his daughter. He was so burned up at this each time he went to their house and pleaded to see his child that he couldn't think straight. He'd roar away angrily and recklessly in his car, get drunk, and soon get picked up by the police as he was heading back to his lonely room.

At the time I saw him he was serving what must have been his seventh or eighth jail sentence. Also by this time he was thinking of using a gun on his ex-wife and in-laws and running off with his little girl.

This sequence of events is not at all infrequent with people who are obsessed with hate and revenge. They are so bent on the destruction of someone else that they can't even see what they are doing to themselves. How much wiser it would have been for our aggrieved father to have forgiven his ex-wife when she was so mean, to do his best to obtain his legal rights, and to lump the whole thing if he couldn't get anywhere!

Stop and think for just one moment how hideous he would have thought someone who forced him to suffer in the way he did. If someone else had kept him awake nights, forced him to drink to excess, jeopardize his job, break the law, get arrested, and wind up having his head examined, do you know what he would have done with that person? He would have used his gun on him. But who actually did that? Why he, himself! All through that whole mess he was his own worst enemy. All along he was insisting his former wife was so mean and unsympathetic to him. In the final analysis he was even more unsympathetic, more uncaring, more damaging to himself than she and her parents were. That's what blame can do to *you*.

Anger can get you electrocuted, jailed for a lifetime, sick to the stomach, and so disinterested in life you can't see anything beautiful anymore. Whoever said revenge was sweet didn't know what he was talking about. Oh, sure, if you can put someone in his place without your losing your composure, that's a different story. The big type of revenge I'm referring to comes only from deep hate, and this is the stuff that can eat you up alive. It is impossible to hate someone without suffering yourself for that hatred. It's like trying to get even with someone by throwing a cactus at him with your bare hands. He may get hurt, to be sure, but so do you. And when you hurt yourself, and don't need to, that's neurotic.

The angry blamer suffers doubly. He suffers the indignities at the hands of his frustraters and he suffers the results of his own neurotic behavior. He doesn't need both. Perhaps he couldn't avoid the first, as the husband in our example had little control over what his ex-in-laws did. However, what he did to himself was monstrously unfair to himself and practically completely avoidable. He had a choice as to what to do. He could have (a) been simply frustrated by his spiteful wife on the one hand, or (b) been frustrated by his spiteful wife and be emotionally disturbed at the same time on the other hand. He chose the latter. Don't you!

Another unhappy consequence of blame is the simple fact that it distracts you from finding a solution to your frustration. While you dream up murder schemes all day (which hardly qualify as solutions to one's problems), the major problem still goes on. That problem may be a sticky one like the above example. It requires cleverness, planning, and a whale of a lot of foxiness. Time and patience might also be required. But how much of this is going to get done by a fellow with his mind on one track, murder?

A humorous example was once given to me by Shirley, a young woman who had continual conflicts with her domineering parents. One night the sparks flew more viciously than usual when Shirley told her folks she did not want to finish college but wanted to work a year or two and then pick up her education. They threatened to cut off all funds, suggested she might not have the privilege of living any longer under their roof, and would not talk to her if she persisted in this wild scheme.

Shirley got so mad over their threats she couldn't think straight. After she quickly told herself neurotic trash like they *couldn't* do this to her, they *had* to see things her way, it was *awful* to have to be frustrated, and they *shouldn't* dominate her because she didn't *want* to be dominated, she stepped outside her house with a spoon and began banging away on a Chinese gong that hung on the porch. This began to attract some attention from the neighbors, but that was nothing compared to the attention she got when she stepped out to the curb and began bouncing that spoon off the hood of the family car. When she saw that this was beginning to have the desired effect on her folks she opened the car door and honked the horn until the police were called.

For all her pains Shirley didn't do one thing to solve her problem, and she wound up in psychotherapy to boot. Her anger completely prevented her from figuring out how she could calm her folks down. With a clear head she could easily have realized that a day or two later she might approach the matter again and probably get better results. Once parents have time to digest an idea they often think better of it. Or, had she contained herself, they would have had to deal with her on an adult and mature level. Instead, by her getting angry they had a child to deal with and their fears were all the more justified.

When you get right down to it, to solve a problem

you must have your mind on solutions, not on the personalities of the persons who are frustrating you. Shirley did not come up with a way out of her dilemma except an unusually emotional one. All she could think of was how unfair her parents were and how they ought to be punished. What did that have to do with finding a way to have them accept her decision to leave school? How did that help her find a way to stay in their good graces so she could receive financial and material aid from them? Obviously it didn't!

Think Twice

Before getting sore the next time something doesn't go your way, think over the damage you could be doing to yourself. This will really take effort and time for you to master, but master it you shall! There is no reason under the sun that you cannot tell yourself that you do not need to have your own way: that it is not for you to say that this world should not be filled with selfish and cruel people simply because you don't want it that way, that people are not bad because they behave badly, and that they should not be dealt with severely because they treat others badly. No matter how tempted you may be to let your blood pressure boil over, remember you are then only adding to your pains and miseries and that that emotional pain is often even worse than the frustration over which you upset yourself. Do not allow yourself to be tempted to walk down that neurotic road of anger, resentment, hatred, or fury. It's an easy step to take, but you'll pay for it dearly sooner or later.

And don't give yourself a lot of bull about how it isn't in your nature to take insults calmly or to sit by calmly while others are being unpleasant. Your so-called nature is nothing more than your habitual way of reacting to frustration. You learned to be that way—you can unlearn to be that way. Just because you've been a roaring bull for most of your life when frustrated, that is no excuse for your roaring like a wounded bull the next time you don't get your way. The past has next to nothing to do with your neurosis today. You get angry today not because you've been a sorehead all your life but because you are still telling yourself that you can't stand not getting your way and that others have no right to be wrong. Should you question these notions the very next time you are frustrated, you will also not get angry the very next time you are frustrated. Try it and see!

6

If Not Anger, What?

O.K., SO BY NOW YOU MAY BELIEVE ME WHEN I SAY you'd be better off not to blame anyone for anything and to keep your cool while you do something else about the problem. But what is that something else? If not anger, what? Should you become a passive coward and let others run all over you? Should you calmly smile at people while they trounce you just so you can boast later about your beautiful mental health? Of course not. Instead, use a number of alternatives to anger.

1. Control Your Own Anger

I know this sounds as if I'm repeating myself, but this is not so obvious as it sounds. The best way to deal with people and their nuttiness is simply to deal with them as calmly as possible. You'd be amazed at how easy it is for others to be calm if they're talking to a calm person. The friendly tone in your voice is the best remedy for the other fellow's wrath. Don't give him reason to strike you and he probably won't. Shoot your mouth off and you give him all the justification he could possibly use to hit back. And isn't that what starts most fights? A person does something you dislike. You get sore over his actions and call him a few choice names. He takes insult from these remarks, and if he wasn't angry before he sure as heck is now. So he clobbers you with a meaner remark or shoves you about or makes some unkind threat. This works you up even more than before, and there you have the makings of a great fight.

Instead of registering anger, try being so nice instead that you completely baffle your frustrater. In fact, follow the advice of Dr. Albert Ellis, the founder of rational-emotive therapy, whose philosophies underlie this book, and be all the nicer to others as they get meaner to you. Do you realize how difficult it is to continue being angry with someone who is being peaches and cream while you're screaming at him? It makes you look foolish. You'd have to be positively out of your mind to continue hating someone who is being nothing but lovely to you. Try it sometime and just see for yourself what a staggering effect it has on most people. Remember, the worse they are to you the nicer you will want to be to them. You will find that anger, like a snowball in the sun, cannot survive for very long.

If you find yourself slipping because your enemy is attacking your mother's biological background, don't fly off the handle. Think of the steps you've already read about and put them into practice. Make yourself say such rational thoughts to yourself as: "He has a right to his views. Everyone has a right to be wrong. I don't *have* to have my way. It *isn't awful* to have him attack my family. Words *don't* hurt." Keep on saying those sensible things until you cool off and can see the other person as a disturbed human being who should have your sympathy, not hate. If that doesn't do the trick, try to fake being cool. Your calmness will have its effect if you give it time. If that doesn't work immediately, it will work the next time perhaps. Some people have to be treated with this approach for a period of time before they feel uncomfortable about themselves and try to grow up.

2. Never Give Up Thinking People Can Control Their Angers

It makes no difference who they are or how long they have practiced their immature habits, people are largely controllable. Make excuses for them because they have red hair, or because they're Irish, or because it's just their nature, and you invite disaster.

I remember a client who told me about her family. Her mother and father often quarreled bitterly until the police had to be called. When the officer stepped through the front door, what do you think greeted him? A scene of rage? A madman? A nut who wanted to throw the policeman out on his ear? Not on your life. The father greeted the officer with the sweetest smile, the friendliest handshake, and an invitation, a chuckle, and an apology for bothering him over a simple family disagreement. In other words, this man, who moments before was pushing his wife around in a most menacing manner, could get hold of himself when he needed, could control himself so well he could act like the perfect gentleman and fool an experienced cop. Invariably the police thought the mother and her daughter were lying.

Anger *can* be controlled unless your brain is literally sick. If you have brain damage from an accident or disease, then, yes, you might be unable to control your violence. However, if you are simply practicing your old habits of insisting on having your way and trying to scare people into giving in to you, then you *can* change that behavior and don't let anyone convince you otherwise.

If your enemy insists he cannot control himself because he has been disturbed in the past and you should make allowances for his neurosis, don't do it. He *can* stop his demandingness. *You've* done it hundreds of times, so why can't he? No one makes a bunch of exceptions for you, so why should you make them for him? If he still argues that point, present him with this hypothetical case: Suppose you were to put a gun against the fellow's head and he knew positively you would blow his brains out if he made one more dirty remark to you. What do you think he would do? He'd be quiet as a church mouse, and you know it. That's what comes from applying yourself and making yourself do something you may not like but of which you are perfectly capable.

This is particularly important in the case of children. If you excuse their angers because they are children, you're asking for it. When you show them how to control anger as I've shown you, then expect more mature behavior of them whether they like it or not. If they tell you about how hard it is, tell them: "Too bad! Keep trying, honey. You'll get better."

Always remember, it takes two to tango. If you won't join in an argument, there will be none. Your accuser may still go on ranting and raving, but that's his problem. As I've said, the calmer you are, the sooner he will probably calm down. But you want to watch out for the bait he will throw your way in the hope you will bite. That bait will be the one choice remark the other fellow will offer because he thinks you can't refuse to react to it.

One woman whose marriage was almost on the rocks told me how her husband could always incite her into a fight. After accusing her of all sorts of nonsense from loafing to infidelity and not finding any of these successful, he would finally call her Shirley, and that would do the trick. Shirley was the name of a woman whom she particularly disliked because she was so selfish with her family and husband. My client could take almost any kind of accusation or teasing but that. And her ever-goading husband knew it.

You do not need to be a victim of this kind of baiting if you watch yourself. Practice control all the time, no matter how badly you do at first. With experience you will get better. If you need to reread these pages over and over, do so. If that doesn't help, seek out a therapist who follows these ideas and let him help point out the weak points in your technique. You do not need to get mad at such baloney, and if you work on it, you won't.

Imagine yourself having an invisible control panel, or rather imagine your husband, parents, or children having one invisibly connected to you. Then imagine what a person could do to you if he knew which buttons to push. Your children usually are past masters at this business of pushing the right buttons to either melt your heart or drive you up the wall. This is invariably true in the case of the power struggle. In this situation the child insists he is more powerful than you, while you insist you are more powerful than he. He therefore watches subconsciously for what is important in your life and when he wants to frustrate you, hoping to anger you, he pushes one of those buttons to which you will react. If he knows it's important to you that he go to college and he must earn good grades to go, he will push the button marked "Stupid" and thus earn poor grades. If he knows you will be worried if he stays out late and he wants to get back at you for making him do dishes the night before, he will push the button marked "Forgetfulness." Then he can always say he forgot what time it was or what time he should have been home, and so on.

You can't win such struggles, so instead of trying to act the policeman to such children let them experience the consequences of their behavior so they can see from their own experiences how right you were. If you are in fact so correct, relax and let their own errors teach them so much more than your sermonizing ever will.

3. Behavior Counts, Not Words

It is what you do about a frustration that counts, not how much you scream your head off over it. Many people would insist that complaining and screaming *is* doing something about a problem, but they're usually wrong. If complaining works, well and good. Too often, however, it does not work and then action is called for. Children and adults can stand complaints and screaming for years and not truly understand just how sincere a person is about his complaints. It sometimes takes only one act to prove what you have been saying for years.

An interesting case is that of Jasper and Louise and his handling of their problem without anger. Louise was frigid with her husband and wanted to leave him a number of times. He protested angrily and sought to make her feel guilty. She stayed with him but had a number of affairs to prove she was not frigid with all men. Jasper knew of these romances and tried to accept them philosophically, and for a time he was able to do that. In time, however, he began to ask himself more seriously if this was truly the way he wanted to live or if he and Louise wouldn't be better off divorced. He decided this was correct and told her his plans. Almost instantly she woke up to what was happening and was amazed that he would actually suggest getting rid of her. When he approached her in that mature and calm way she knew he wasn't bluffing. That night they had a long talk about their past marriage and the good times they had in contrast to the bad, and through many tears and apologies they both reconsidered their moves and fell in love again. This time Louise was not frigid and never has been again.

Such is the power of actions over words.

With children, the difference between getting along and constantly screaming at them rests almost entirely in the technique of substituting action for scoldings. Pat, a teen-age girl, hated to bathe. Her mother wasted breath, composure, and energy on her daughter. Finally, at my suggestion, she told Pat the kitchen table would be out of bounds to her until she came to the table clean. Otherwise she could eat whatever she found in the refrigerator and eat it in the bathroom or basement.

You must admit this is a nice example of firmness over anger. Pat, however, took it badly and spitefully refused to eat for two days. On top of that she developed a cold, took cold medicine, threw up because of the weakened condition of her stomach, and kept this up until her stomach was sore. For this she received her mother's sympathy but not a change in policy. Finally, seeing she had a great deal to lose by pigheadedly sticking with her policy, Pat gave in and took regular baths from then on.

4. Watch Out for Control Strategies

The moment you become firm with anyone he will attempt to do something to remove that frustration. If one approach does not work, he will try another. Count on it. Man is amazingly creative when it comes to getting his way, and nowhere is that creativity better displayed than in dealing with human obstacles to one's desires. Especially amazing is the creativity shown by children in getting around frustrations. There should be an award of the year to the child with the most ingenious scheme for getting around an irritating and frustrating parent. He or she would have every right to prize it like an Oscar. Such is the height to which this art can sometimes reach.

A typical example of strategies used in a family is the case of the Hogans. The kids had practically taken over the house with the cooperation of their mother, who did not spend much time cleaning up after them and who allowed their friends in the house all day and even late into the night. The teen-age daughter was in the habit of having her boyfriend drop in after ten in the evening, when Mr. Hogan felt inclined to walk around the house in his pajamas. To make things even cozier, at the daughter's insistence the mother agreed to pick up the boyfriend and take him to school when she chauffeured her daughter, even though he had his own ride. They enjoyed being together, it seems.

One fine day this mess hit the fan. Mr. Hogan had had enough and put his foot down. But he yelled, threatened, and even swatted the kids a few times when they smarted off to him. In no time at all his wife and the children came back with so many guilt-provoking strategies and utterances of self-righteous indignation that he caved in and let things fall back to where they were before he complained.

In counseling, however, he later learned that these strategies are simple schemes people use to gain their own ends, and as such are perfectly normal and to be expected when we put obstacles in the way of other people's satisfactions. I reminded him that he had better predict which schemes he might encounter the next time he made a ruling in the home and thereby not be surprised and overwhelmed. He predicted she'd get angry and yell, nothing more. This is what she had always done, and he could see no reason why she would do differently next time.

He was advised to go home, to tell the family what he expected of them and that he fully expected his wife to back him up. Then he was to sit back calmly and watch the fireworks and make notes as to who was reacting and how. This he did, and below is a step-by-step analysis of his wife's reactions.

Mr. Hogan told his wife she was not to pick up their daughter's boyfriend any longer; that he wanted more privacy around the house; that there would be a curfew during the week of 9:00 P.M., when it was to be expected that all the visiting kids would be asked to leave; and finally, he did not want to see the house in as constant a mess as he was accustomed to seeing it.

Well, he was right. His wife hit the ceiling. Thirty minutes later she came down to earth for air and let him have it again. That was strategy number one.

Naturally she expected this plan to work because it always had worked. That's why, when asked what his wife would do if frustrated, Mr. Hogan had suggested she would get angry but did not elaborate as to what she might do if that tactic did not work. In all of their years of marriage she seldom *needed* to go beyond this first step because it worked well enough.

Strategy number two came into play several days later when her third anger outburst did not move her husband. That's when she began to cry. She claimed she felt abused, she had no rights, he was always getting his way, all she ever wanted was to have her children contented to be home and happy, and what was so wrong (sniff, sniff) with that?

The old boy almost weakened with that one, but luckily I had prepared him well for that possibility, so he again calmly stated the kids had to go, the house had to be kept clean, and the boyfriend would not be picked up and transported to school at their expense.

Strategy number three was a threat of suicide. This came a few days later when the second tactic failed. "I might as well kill myself if I'm not going to have some happiness in my own home. I couldn't possibly live with a dictator. Death is better than a life of slavery. Why should I go on and get no thanks for my efforts? If that's all life with you is going to be, who needs it?" And so it went for another while. But my client had learned his lesson well. He remained firm, cool, and detached. He was fighting for his family and his own happiness and knew that if he let things slide back to the way they had been, he would reject them and that would be bad for all concerned. So he sweated out this strategy and took on the next one.

In strategy number four she decided she would leave him. Her mother lived across town and could put her and the children up until they could locate better quarters. He could stay in the house, but would he support her and the children? Yes? Fine! If he wanted to divorce her, she would understand. Then too, perhaps she ought to obtain the divorce. Wasn't she the grieved party? She was? Then he could understand her feeling as she did? Well!

The fourth strategy clearly wasn't going to work, so all that was left in her bag of tricks was number five: kill him! He deserved to die, so inhuman was he. The children and she would be better off without him. It didn't matter that she might be arrested, she would be released once the courts really knew what she had to put up with. And, because she was so wrought up, he ought to sleep in a separate room, because he would never know if she might not walk in her sleep and konk him over the head.

By this time Mr. Hogan was in complete control and calmly watched the strategies roll by. Now he could clearly see them for what they were: devices, schemes, games his wife was playing to get her way. If, incidentally, he had felt anywhere along the way she might have done what she threatened, he knew he would have to remain firm and let it happen. If she looked as though she would really kill herself over this issue, he was instructed to hospitalize her immediately. If he came on the scene too late, too bad. It would not be his fault, and he would not have driven her to it. *She* would clearly have been responsible for her own death, not he. No one drives you to suicide by denying you such simple wishes. Also, no one can upset others, only frustrate them. Ms. Hogan would have been quite guilty of upsetting herself very neurotically, and her suicide would have been her fault, not her husband's.

More importantly, had he given in to her suicidal threats he would indirectly have encouraged her to try those threats again in the future. This way, by ignoring them and taking a reasonable risk, he showed her once and for all he would not succumb to these tactics and she would simply have to come up with a better solution.

Which is what she eventually did, but not until she got through strategy number six. This was the apple-polishing approach and went as follows: "Honey, I'm sorry for the way I've acted. Surely we can reach some settlement on this matter. I'm certain you wouldn't mind the children having their friends over during the weekends if they help clean up before they leave. I can see where you've resented the wear and tear on the furniture, but that would take care of the matter. And if Suzie's boyfriend offered to bring her home sometimes, wouldn't that be fair?"

This is an important step where firmness may begin to crumble because it all sounds so decent and reasonable. Mr. Hogan was taught to expect this step too, however, and was ready for it. He thought over her proposal very carefully and found it full of holes and in no way actually curative of the ills he found in the family. For one thing, he wasn't interested in getting the kids out of the home only because it would save wear and tear on the furniture. It was also to get the kids playing outside, plus teaching their friends they owed something to his family to share the responsibilities of entertaining. Why should it always be his soda pop that was drunk or his cookies that were being consumed by the bagful? Didn't the parents of those other kids see the unfairness?

As for having the children over only on the weekends, that wasn't the point either. He didn't mind their being over during the week, for that matter—he just didn't want them over all day and night. His children had chores and homework to do and their musical instruments to practice as well. With all that company these things could not easily be done. And then, of course, there was the matter of the infringement on his privacy, an issue that became more and more irritating the longer it went on. He could stand having people over sometimes, but having his privacy invaded practically all the time from after supper to bedtime, that was something else. Two nights a week of their company was enough!

The last concession his wife wanted him to make he also contested. The boyfriend had always had rides available to school because he had a car pool which could have brought him to school in the morning. It wasn't until he got serious with Suzie that he no longer took advantage of that arrangement. Mr. Hogan disapproved, not only of his car being used to chauffeur this fellow around, but even more the great closeness developing between this boy and his daughter. Ms. Hogan didn't mind this, but Mr. Hogan did. It was the central issue of the chauffeuring, not the driving itself.

The upshot of this whole matter was that Ms. Hogan finally had to sit down and calmly listen to what her husband was troubled over. They arrived at an arrangement each could live with, and they did it without any dissolution of the marriage. That's what can happen if you are aware of the series of maneuvers you're likely to encounter when you frustrate someone.

5. Analyze the Accusation

The way to handle accusations of any kind is to do what Dr. Albert Ellis does. He advises us to look at two alternatives when we are accused of something. The first is, "Is it true?" and the second is, "Is it false?"

If the accusation is true, then admit it without shame or guilt. You are after all a human being who has a right to millions of faults, and the one you were just accused of is merely one of them. To get insulted over being accused of being imperfect is silly, since all of us come short of perfection, including that lovable person doing the accusing. If you are a dirty old man and someone accuses you of being one, relax. If you know you're one and don't mind it, why get upset? The same would be true if you were accused of being cheap. If it was true and you knew it was, and you didn't mind being frugal, why react to the accusation? You've apparently found a life-style you're content with, so why defend it just because someone else finds fault with it? You surely wouldn't get disturbed if someone accused you of being a Democrat if that was the case. You'd say to yourself: "Yes, I'm a Democrat. That fellow apparently disapproves of Democrats, but I don't. Nevertheless, he's correct, so what am I getting hot under the collar for?"

If the accusation is true and you disapprove of the accusation because you didn't know you were what you were accused of, then admit it and thank your accuser for being so honest and having the kindness to tell you that you were acting like a dirty old man at the party last night, that you have body odor, or that you've been acting like a skinflint lately. You too disapprove of these actions, so be grateful to your accuser for being honest enough to tell you you're overly sexy, smelly, or cheap. If it's true it's true, and it's a good thing someone had the courage to tell you the truth.

In the event, however, that the accusation is obviously not true, what does Dr. Ellis then advise us to do? Why, give the other fellow the right to his opinion and let the matter rest there. For example, doesn't he have the right to think you're a dirty old man? If that's the way he sees your harmless kidding with the office staff, that's his problem. If he can't stand your brand of cologne and thinks you smell awful, that's his problem. And if he cannot see why you don't spend more lavishly considering your good wages, that's none of his business and again that's *his* problem. As Dr. Ellis so aptly puts it, "He's got rocks in *his* head," and he has a right to them. In this way it is possible never to become upset over any accusation or to *make* insults out of unkind remarks. In the final analysis we cannot be insulted unless we *make* an insult of a remark. It is always we, not others, who insult us. It is your supersensitive interpretation and your highly personal way of reacting to others that converts their harmless comments into stinging insults.

You can also think of this difference of opinion's being no different than any other difference of opinion. If that same fellow who accused you of all these things was to attend a movie with you and you stated that you enjoyed the show while he stated it was an awful show, would you get insulted and angry? No? Of course you wouldn't, but why not? Isn't it simply because you'd allow him to have his opinion without thinking he had to agree with yours? Well, if you two can disagree peacefully over a movie, why can't the two of you also disagree peacefully over whether you smell, are cheap, or are a lecherous old girl chaser?

6. Enforce Logical Consequences

Unless you suffer for your mistakes you're likely to continue making them. If others let you get off scot-free when you have behaved badly, you will act badly again in the belief nothing uncomfortable will happen to you.

Some years ago I was the director of a mental health center, and a young man was sent to us for study. His girl had gone out one Saturday night with another fellow. He became so enraged he got his dad's gun and shot it off up and down the main street of a small town. The police thought he was disturbed, so they brought him in as a supposed psychiatric case. One of my staff gave him a diagnosis and recommended he be allowed to return home under the provision he be ordered into psychotherapy.

I was shocked at his total disregard of what that young man had almost done. He had walked up the main street of a town a bit tipsy, blasted away with a dangerous weapon and just luckily not injured anyone, and my colleague wanted to put him on a couch and let him tell us what a sad thing it was not to go out with his honeybunch last Saturday night. Not on your life! He had lost complete control of himself and felt awfully sorry for himself to boot. So, tough! Should we die or be injured for this minor frustration in his life? Isn't it high time instead that lover boy learns to accept disappointments in a mature way and take it on the chin? I have to do that every week, and so do you and so did my staff. Yet when it came to their thinking about this fellow in a mature way they went completely soft in the head.

What this boy needed was a short stay in the county jail and after he had a good taste of that, then to be sent to the mental health worker to teach him how to avoid that sort of relapse of control again. He couldn't be blamed for the incident in the first place since he obviously didn't know how to control his emotions. Therapy could teach him that. But jail, or something equally frustrating, was the only thing capable of teaching him he *needed* therapy. Until he recognized he had a bad problem he would be under the opinion (*a*) that other people disturb him, (*b*) that it is awful to be frustrated, (*c*) that people shouldn't frustrate him, and (*d*) if they do, they are bad and need punishment.

Those of you who would argue that this is what we seem to have been doing all these years with our prison systems are ignoring the fact that our prisons punish much more than the crime deserves, that a man is blamed for frustrating society, and society fights him because it regards him as bad and in need of suffering. Society with its unfeeling prisons and long prison terms has become no different than the person it is punishing. Both have lost their perspectives and hearts! Only when anger and revenge enter into the picture are we guilty of worse behavior than they committed whom we seek to correct.

Among the major issues adults get angry over are their children. Using logical consequences to discipline them is so much better than physical punishment or shouting, that some remarks will have to be made to cover that technique as it applies to youngsters.

If your son touches a hot stove, he gets burned and learns to leave it alone. The burning is a *natural* consequence of touching a hot stove. Being bitten by a mean dog because he threw a stone at him, or climbing out too far on a weak limb and falling are also typical examples of natural consequences. Because these consequences can hurt like the very dickens the child learns very quickly not to touch hot objects, throw stones at dogs, or climb out on weak branches.

Nothing personal is suggested in these penalties. The hot stove burned your boy because it was hot, not because it thought your boy was bad and needed punishment. The dog was also only doing what all mean dogs do when hit with stones. And the weak limb did not resent the boy climbing on it and then break to punish him. It broke because it was weak and would have broken at any time if enough weight was placed on it.

121

In short, a natural consequence teaches its lessons very well because the child knows nothing personal was meant when he got hurt. He can either accept things the painful way they are and avoid them or he can fool with them and get hurt. If he's sensible, he learns to avoid them.

Now suppose your son comes home at one A.M. and was supposed to be in by midnight. Do you want to give him a sermon and tell him where he erred for the umpteenth time or is there something better to do? Fortunately there are *logical* consequences. These are the consequences that follow sensibly, not haphazardly, from previous actions.

For instance, if you make your son scrub the kitchen floor at one A.M. for coming in late and you try to tell him you're only doing that to teach him to get in on time, he'll not believe you. Why not? Because he can see no reasonable connection between scrubbing the floor and getting in earlier. He'll interpret that action as an act of revenge of your part, and he'll be right. Naturally he will not cooperate with you or learn from the experience if he figures you're doing it only to make him suffer.

Now suppose you told him you would lock the front door at midnight, and that if he wanted to sleep at home that night he would have to get in on time or sleep elsewhere. And suppose you explained with logical arguments that you'd be in bed by that time and wouldn't want to be awakened by his late arrival. Furthermore, you wouldn't want to leave the door unlocked since a thief could open the door easily enough.

Suppose you gave your child this kind of situation. What would happen? Well, if he came home on time, all would be well and good. But if he came home after midnight and found the house quiet and securely bolted and no one coming to let him in, he would realize he made that choice to be locked out, and he couldn't hold you blameworthy for his inconvenience. At least that's the argument you would have to answer his protests.

"Son, if you want to sleep in your room, you know how to accomplish that. Come home on time. However, if it's very important for you to stay out past midnight, I won't blame you. But don't expect me to spoil my sleep. I have to go to work in the morning and I can't get back to sleep for hours if I once wake up after I'm in bed. The choice is yours. I'm not saying you have to do one or the other. You make up your mind which you prefer, and you live with either consequence."

Notice how the father has gotten off his son's back. He is no longer the villain. He has turned the matter over to his son to decide and is content to live with his decision.

Some of the more common issues with kids and the logical consequences I have found work well are the following:

a. Not being in by curfew. Tell the child he may be picked up by the police and jailed, but that you will not bail him out if he makes the choice to defy the law. The choice is his.

b. Your child will not shut off his desk lamp in tne morning before going to school. Go in and dismantle the lamp, unplug it from the socket, and use the argument that you thought something must have been wrong with it since it wasn't shut off. He'll know you don't mean that, but he will get the message that he'd better switch the light off or he'll have to assemble it in the evening.

The same can be done for a radio left blaring in a room vacated by the child. Move the bed or desk if necessary, unplug the radio, wrap the cord around it, and lay it on the bed. The consequence for not shutting it off is having to move the bed and plug it in at a time when he comes home tired and wants to relax. And what's so logical about doing that? Why simply to recover some of the lost electricity that was wasted when he wasn't in the room to listen to it. Now he has to take some time to set the radio up again.

c. The child fights over doing the dishes. Fine! Tell him he does not need to eat at your table if it's very important to him not to clean the dishes. You don't care much either way what he does. The choice is his. Either do the dishes and enjoy good food or get out of a boring job but scrounge through the refrigerator.

d. The youngster will not put his seat belt on while the car is moving. Instead of yelling at him and possibly endangering both your lives, give him a choice again. The logical consequence of the belt's being unbuckled is that the car pulls off to the side of the road and stops. When the belt is buckled again, the car almost automatically and without a word from the driver merges into the traffic again.

e. What to do about the child who will not eat with his utensils? Give him a choice. Eat with a knife and fork or eat with his fingers. Once he tries mashed potatoes and gravy, or gelatin, he'll see quickly enough the advantage tools have over fingers.

f. Leaving toys and clothing lying around on the floor and furniture. Obviously there is only one thing to do. Pick up these items and put them away for a week. Soon he'll learn that if he wants his things he'll have to store them when he's through or they mysteriously disappear.

g. Talking or fighting among brothers and sisters while watching TV. Shut off the set without saying a word.

124

The moment things are quiet again, the set goes on. Surely they cannot fail to comprehend the logical consequence of being loud while the family views television.

h. The children will not take their dirty clothes to the laundry room. Fine—don't you go to their rooms and collect them. If they aren't interested enough in having clean clothes, let them use up all they have until one fine day they want a special article and realize they have no clean clothes. They'll run to the laundry room with their arms full of dirty clothes, I can assure you.

I could go on and on. But the point has been made. As Rudolf Dreikurs so wisely reminded us, we parents preach, sermonize, and lecture far too much. If we would tell the child more often what the consequences will be if he does such and such, and then back off and let him make his own choice, he may sometimes get hurt, to be sure. But the hurt and training he gets by our screaming angrily at him all the time isn't doing him much good either.

7. Teach Others What You Have Learned

Most of the time you cannot teach anyone anything when he is in the heat of an argument. You usually want to wait until things have cooled off a bit, but not too much. While you're debating with each other you're in a good position to teach others what you have learned about anger.

The first thing you want to educate them to is that you did not upset them as they are probably insisting. They'll tell you you're wrong and off your rocker, but do not be dissuaded. You're right, by George, and they're wrong! Explain to them how their thinking, not your actions, upsets them and that if they don't know how to change their irrational thoughts to rational thoughts they should go to a psychotherapist. You learned how not to anger yourself—they can learn it too.

Another important fact to teach angry people is that blowing off steam isn't always all *that* healthy. In fact, there can be real danger in letting your feelings come to the surface. If they argue that they could develop many physical symptoms if they bottled up their angers, tell them that *might* happen if they did that chronically. If they insist on letting their feelings be known, well and good, only should they use blame and force in the process of airing their feelings? No one deserves either. If they want to assert themselves in a firm but kind way, well and good. If they cannot do that, advise them to keep their neurotic and dangerous impulses to themselves. Why should all of us suffer just because they want the childish delight of giving vent to their impulses? I don't want to lose a tooth or an eye because some emotional baby has gotten himself mad and thinks the world should be shaped according to his demands. As I didn't do anything wrong, let him suffer, not me!

This business of giving vent to your resentments is the old ventilation theory of aggression. That theory says that we have to become aggressive if we are frustrated. Now we know this is nonsense, because all of us are often frustrated and often we lump it and don't become angry. It's true, of course, that ventilating your fury can be helpful and even healthy if it is done in a safe way. Chop down a tree, run around the block, or make a drawing of someone driving a dagger through your enemy's heart and you may well feel better and no one is the worse for wear. Better still, however, why get angry in the first place so that ventilation is required? Wouldn't it be better to talk yourself *out* of anger instead of trying

126

to release it harmlessly after you have got yourself in that state? It *can* be done, and that's what this book is all about.

The most impressive example of the futility of ventilation to relieve hostility came to me years ago when this technique was in vogue among us psychotherapists. The case was not mine but my colleague's. He had seen weekly for about one year a young woman in her twenties who harbored great anger toward her mother. Every Monday at two o'clock, as regular as clockwork, she would come into his office, spill out her resentments for a whole hour, and tell him how she imagined her mother roasting in hell and all sorts of other fiendish delights, and feel wonderful when she left. At first the therapist was thrilled with the open way this girl expressed herself, but after hearing fifty variations on the same theme he soon fell asleep behind the sunglasses he had learned to wear in self-defense.

Not once in all those sessions did she ever learn to talk herself out of being angry. That idea was not even accepted yet professionally. The therapist honestly believed he was helping the woman because she always came back for more. She felt much better when she left, but somehow the realization that she never got over her anger escaped him.

8. Never Forget How Neurotic Most People Are

You cannot be seriously angry with most people if you fully understand how little they can help their behavior because they are so truly neurotic. Just as you would not take personally the rantings and ravings of anyone clearly out of his mind, so too you can avoid overreacting to those who are merely miffed. They too are suffering emo-

127

tional disturbances, even when their gripes are over petty issues. One woman I counseled, for example, was among the most miserable I had ever encountered. She yelled at her family almost every day for the most inconsequential matters: The light was on in the closet; the light was off in the hallway; the refrigerator was left open too long; the freezer should have been defrosted yesterday; Johnny didn't make his bed before leaving for school that morning; Cindy took too long to get out into the kitchen for her breakfast. How that normal family could tolerate that bickering and whining for all those years was a marvel. It was not they, however, who sought me out for counseling—it was Mamma. She wanted to know what she could do about her inconsiderate family which was slowly driving her nuts! How ironic! She did need my help for the reasons she could not yet imagine.

The family followed the Biblical teaching of turning the other cheek. Once they learned to control their angers she had no control over them, so she became harmless. And why get mad at a harmless person? Instead, they treated her kindly and increased this as she became more frustrating. Her yelling was no match for their serenity, and it drove her to counseling.

Another favorite trick of neurotically angry people is the double bind. In this situation you can't win if you follow their advice and you can't win if you don't. Typical of this maneuver is the husband who wants his wife to help him paint the kitchen. He soon criticizes her for the way she is doing it and tells her to stop and let him finish by himself. When he realizes what he had gotten himself into, he lambastes her for being uncooperative and making him work alone. That's the kind of talk that can literally drive you insane if you let it. And the best way to fight it is to realize that anyone who puts you in

128

such a spot is quite literally disturbed and cannot be taken seriously. Consider the source next time and do what *you* think is right.

Recently I had group therapy with about twelve clients. Fully half of them were there because they could not handle their neurotic parents. One client had a nervous tic, another attempted suicide several times, and a few others escaped into drugs. All were also furious at the impossible behavior of their mothers or fathers or both.

They all unthinkingly insisted their parents should not treat them as they had. I attempted to show them, however, that neurotic parents *must* act neurotically—they have no choice. In addition, my clients did not need to take such behavior personally since these parents would behave in that manner whether it was toward my client or not. A disturbed person must and will behave as though he is disturbed. That's how I explained to my angry clients that one's mother could not help threatening suicide if her son went off to marry, or that another's father became crude and vulgar when he drank. Worst of all, these neurotic parents usually try their best to get their kids brainwashed into thinking it is they—the children—who are the screwballs, not the parents.

You cannot be surprised or angered at any neurotic behavior when you truly accept the fact that your parents (and everyone else for that matter) are irrational some of the time and some of them are upset a great deal of the time. That may not be a nice way to view one's parents, but if they are neurotic they are neurotic. Hiding from the truth is foolish. This does not justify our getting angry with them, because they cannot help their weaknesses and disturbances. They are loving and caring people even though they are rocky in the head at times. If we forgive them their weaknesses, they may be able to forgive us ours.

Adolescents and young adults can be particularly alert to this situation. Unless they learn to look upon their parents in an objective and honest fashion they will invariably believe the claptrap those sick people push into their heads. Then the world will be cursed with another generation of neurotics.

Another point to bear in mind about forgiveness is this: sooner or later we usually forgive those we argue with. Only very disturbed people hold grudges forever. Therefore, since you are likely to forgive your frustrater sometime, perhaps in fifteen days, then make every effort to do it in the first fifteen minutes and spare yourself a great deal of sullen suffering. And don't fool yourself about how impossible that is. It *is* possible if you just see how sensible the above point is.

9. Count to Ten

As corny as this may sound, the method nevertheless has merit. It will not of course prevent you from thinking angrily (only challenging the idea that you must have your way can do that). But it will aid you in controlling your anger long enough to prevent you from putting your foot into your mouth and will give you time to collect your thoughts.

One of our past Presidents had a press secretary who repeatedly used this delaying tactic so he wouldn't blurt out something to an annoying reporter and possibly embarrass the President. If counting to ten didn't help, he would look at something handy, such as a matchbook, and examine it carefully. This distracted his thoughts just enough to enable him to avoid building up his angry feelings into embarrassing outbursts.

Unfortunately he did not know what caused anger to begin with, or he could have talked himself out of those feelings readily enough. Instead of thinking a reporter had no right to ask this question or make that remark, he would have been better off to remind himself instantly that people cannot upset him with words, that they have a right to their views, and that they even have the right to ask impolite and probing questions.

He didn't know all this but he did reasonably well by counting to ten instead. In all the years he was the President's press secretary I was never aware of his ever showing any more than minor feelings of annoyance.

7

Making It Work

HELP FOR YOUR TEMPER IS ALL AROUND, THOUGH YOU may never find it. This is especially true if you expect to get help through the usual channels open to you in the past: some forms of therapy and institutions. These sources have not dealt with everyday anger adequately at all. To find help for your ordinary temper outbursts as well as for your rare violent ones you will have to look to a new form of therapy which has become increasingly popular in the last ten years: rational-emotive therapy (RET).

What I have explained in this book is based largely on RET teachings. These teachings are so unique and practical that I felt I could write a book on an age-old subject without repeating very much of what had been said before. In addition, because RET claims we upset ourselves by the irrational ideas we tell ourselves, it makes sense that anger can be overcome by teaching us how to identify these irrational ideas and what to replace them with. And this *can* be taught! It is perfectly possible for many of you to learn better control of your angers merely from reading this book. Unfortunately some of your angers may not be affected at all, and in that case you will want to get counseling to receive help with the particularly difficult problems.

And what should you expect from good counseling? The same thing you have been getting all your life from people whom you have respected. Unfortunately, however, you have had a number of bad teachers throughout the years, and that is why you have emotional problems. Do not think you are disturbed because you couldn't learn to be more stable. The fact that you are disturbed indicates only that you learned your lessons very well but the lessons were foolish ones, taught by persons who meant well but were themselves all messed up in important ways. This means that if you had the capacity to learn to think neurotically, you can learn to think rationally *if* you have a teacher who knows what he is talking about. How do you find such a person? Observe your teacher or therapist and see if he can do what he is trying to teach you. If he can't control his angers any better than you, you can figure him for being just as ignorant on the subject as you are and send *him* to counseling. If you can find someone who has got angry only once in several years, that's your man.

No matter how much he teaches you about your angers, he can only do so much and no more. The rest of the task is up to you. To make the most of his and your efforts you want to be aware of several problems you are likely to run into which could hamper your progress.

Don't Get Discouraged

Some of you will find that control and elimination of anger will come remarkably easily merely from the first reading of this book. You're the lucky ones. Others will find their habit of reacting impulsively and bitterly so strong they will repeat their angry scenes over and over again. This is the more usual case. Be sure not to blame yourself for your early failures (or any failures, for that matter) and get right back to analyzing what you did incorrectly.

If you stop and think over what you were telling yourself after each incidence of anger, you will usually find that you said a number of things. Some of these thoughts will be sensible and healthy, while some will be irrational and neurotic. It is the latter thoughts that you will want to detect so that you can talk yourself out of believing that trash. When you then attack those irrational beliefs to the point where you do not believe them any longer, your anger will have to lift like fog.

For instance, a client recently came to me in some distress, saying she was feeling intense anger but didn't have the slightest idea as to why she should feel this way. It came on the day before, when she saw a young woman push her daughter impatiently through the door of a supermarket because the child was dawdling and the mother had her arms full of shopping bags. When questioned as to why she would be so furious at a strange woman who was behaving fairly normally under the circumstances, she was blank. I instructed her to think aloud and attempt to make some sense of this, even if she had to guess.

"Well," she mused, "the woman probably reminded me of my sister whom I've been thinking of lately because we have been trying to settle Mother's estate, and I'm afraid I'll get a pushing around from her as I have always gotten ever since we were kids."

"Then do you suppose the sight of that mother pushing the girl angrily through the door reminded you of your pushy sister and what she's likely to do to you?" I asked.

"Yes, I'm sure it is now. It even makes me boil inside now just to think of it."

"O.K., then tell me what you're telling yourself that's making you angry."

"The first thing that comes to my mind is that I'm going to take a pushing around by my sister. Could that explain my anger?"

"No, it could not since that's not an irrational idea. You see, it *is* quite possible that you may take some dominating from her through this affair. Sensible thoughts do not disturb you, only irrational, senseless, silly ideas can upset you."

She thought a bit longer. "We'll get into a fight, I'm almost certain. That would account for my hateful feeling toward that woman, wouldn't it?"

"Sorry, wrong again. That idea makes sense too. From your past experience I'd say you had an excellent chance of getting into a real row with your sister when it comes to settling the estate. And because that's a true statement, it also cannot account for your angry feeling."

"I give up. What am I telling myself that's making me angry?"

"That she *can't* frustrate you. That you *must* have your sister behave as you would like her to behave. That she's a *bad person* for behaving badly and therefore she *deserves* to be punished. Now those ideas are all irrational, every last one of them, because you cannot prove they make sense. For instance, your sister *can* and *will* frustrate you whether you deserve it or not. Secondly, she does *not* have to do as you like because you *don't* have to have your way even if you're right. And if she is totally selfish and mean, she still isn't a bad person, only a disturbed one, and beating her to a pulp isn't going to make a lovable and fair creature out of her.

"These are your irrational ideas, and the sooner you will challenge them until you see them for the neurotic nonsense they are, the sooner you will be calmed."

It took my client quite a while before she could get over these notions, but in time she did. At first she thought I was an idiot for suggesting she was totally wrong on each of these counts, but as we debated the issues and as she persisted in coming back for more sessions and more clarification she too could begin to realize she didn't run the world and that her sister had a right to her views. This process took some months before it turned this angry woman into a smiling person, but her perseverance finally paid off. If you give up too soon, you will do yourself a disservice. When you try to challenge neurotic thoughts and you still find yourself angry, *debate some more*. Keep it up until you actually talk yourself out of believing them. Even if you only say the right words without being at all convinced of them, it's a start at least. I guarantee that you will talk yourself out of those absurd ideas you were taught all your life if you question over and over the beliefs you were told were so true.

Discipline Yourself

You may not enjoy shutting your mouth when what you really want to do is shoot it off, but for your health and the health of others it is better in the long run that you do so. Blow up in haste and cool off at leisure is the sad tale being learned by millions of people throughout the world. Yet learning self-discipline, no matter how hard it may be initially, is still much easier than sitting it out in prison for fifty years. So bite your lips or dig your fingernails into your palms, because holding yourself back will be easier on you than expressing cruel hostility will be. To do this you must get over another neurotic notion which invariably leads to poor self-discipline: the idea that it is easier to avoid a difficult task than it is to face it.

This is clearly an absurd idea, as everyone would agree, but we find it difficult to follow. Most of us are very disciplined in many areas of our lives but we each have some chores we hate to get to. For me it's cutting the lawn, and because I put off each week what could take me only an hour, I sometimes have to work three hot hours cutting grass that looks like a wheat field. In practically every other area of my life, however, I am really quite disciplined.

You too are full of willpower in most things, but you also have your weak points. If anger is one of them, watch out—it could kill you. Blurt out the wrong word to the right person and you could be chewing on all of your teeth. Allow yourself the privilege of telling your silly boss just what a fool you really think he is and you'll feel marvelous for five minutes and maybe even for five days. Once that beautiful mood wears off, however, you'll wish dearly you had kept your mouth shut so you could still be working and bringing home the bread.

To acquire self-discipline requires the realization that difficult tasks are better handled by facing them (regardless of how ugly and difficult they may be) than by avoiding them. Controlling your anger is sometimes among the most difficult acts you can perform. Be that as it may, do it! It will be the easier of the two directions you could take. If you end up giving in to your habit of

137

getting angry, you thereby strengthen it. When you eventually get around to wanting to control it the habit will be all the stronger.

This advice does not apply to those instances when you feel you want to pretend anger because it would be highly efficient to do so. With children you will find these ideas particularly applicable, because kids can be very obnoxious and stubborn. The harder you push them, the worse they behave. Soon you may find yourself in a power struggle which can get more devastating than you'd believe. You will be trying to show your child you are more powerful than he or she, and the child will be trying to prove he or she is more powerful than you. What you don't know is that the child is right. Children don't care what they must do to win such a contest so they play dirty, hit below the belt, so to speak, and play by such an unfair set of rules you couldn't possibly follow them. A power struggle with a child is always handled best if you do not engage in the struggle. Pull out of it completely. Let the child suffer with his mistakes. That's the pressure which will eventually change his behavior—not your anger.

You Don't Need to Make Matters Worse

The last thing you need in this world after someone has done you an injustice is to do a greater injustice to yourself. Getting angrily upset over a frustration does not usually remove the frustration and always adds to your discomfort. In fact, most of the time the greatest distress comes not from what others do to us but from what we let our upsets do.

If we would be more calm in response to an insult, for

instance, we would only have to bear the indignity of the mean remark. That is already unpleasant enough. To get furious over the dumb remark, however, makes your discomfort perhaps ten times greater. Therefore, if you would be kind to yourself, keep your disturbances down to a minimum and you thereby do yourself an enormous amount of good.

There are two statements I usually make to myself which help me keep my cool. The first is that I am not God and am neurotic to insist I have to have my way. This usually cools me off nicely. However, if that doesn't do the trick, I always throw in this next thought. "Hauck, be smart, someone is trying to shaft you. That's bad enough, old boy. Surely you're not going to be dumb now and do to yourself what that fellow is trying to do. No, sir! Maybe he doesn't give a hoot about my feelings, but I sure do. Therefore, I'm going to forcibly talk myself out of the angry mood which is beginning to come over me. Having trouble is one thing, and it's often unavoidable. But making *double trouble* for myself is another matter entirely."

I don't always have to go through that long spiel each time I want to calm my budding wrath. Now, in fact, I merely have to think of the great pain in the neck I'd be giving myself and how I sure don't want anyone going around smirking and chuckling about how he got to me, and I manage a fair degree of tranquillity.

Always remember, the neurotic reaction is almost invariably worse by far than an injustice. If the injustice happens to be an immense one, it still doesn't make any sense to get disturbed and make things worse.

The one exception to controlling your anger is in self-defense. When your life is at stake you might be better off keeping your wits about you to be a more efficient antagonist. If you cannot do this, don't worry about it. Hit back as hard as you can. The little damage your neurotic anger can do you at that moment is nothing compared to the damage the other person might inflict on you. Self-defense is the most important issue at the moment, not your anger. It is even conceivable that being angry and very uncontrolled might scare your opponent or give you strength you would not have if you deliberately tried to be too rational.

Anger Against Yourself

Never forget that all I have said about the other fellow applies to you also. As a member of the human race you are no different in your essential qualities than he. This means that not only can you become unreasonably angry with others, you can also hate yourself, resent yourself, and beat yourself. To some extent we are all masochists, people who punish themselves and perhaps even enjoy the pain. The most common reason for hating yourself is that you judge yourself by your actions just as you hate others when you judge them by their actions. The results of this process are that you will show several serious personality symptoms, depression being among the most serious. Self-blame is only one way in which you can depress yourself, but it is one of the most painful. It is no different from other-blame, except for the direction. Otherwise the consequences are identical. Hate others and you'll want to punish them. Hate yourself and you'll punish yourself. You can punish yourself by literally beating your body or whipping yourself. Or you might burn yourself with cigarettes, cut yourself with knives or razors, marry a bum, or deliberately but unconsciously convince yourself you can't do a job and then allow yourself to fail by default. In general you can be a loser in life because how else could you punish yourself better than that?

This would all be unnecessary if you were not angry with yourself. You never deserve blame any more than others do. You are an acceptable person (to yourself at least) regardless of how badly you perform. If you never judge yourself by your actions, you will never feel vain or inferior. The benefits of overcoming anger are twofold, therefore—you will be a nicer companion to others and you will be a nicer companion to yourself. That is why we often see hostility and depression together occurring often from self-blame. When you blame others you become hostile and angry. When you blame yourself you become depressed and feel inferior.

Simple but Not Easy

I received a book review recently from my publisher on my book *Overcoming Depression*. The reviewer had mentioned that I had made the matter of controlling depression oversimplified. He thereby implied that I did not know what I was talking about and that I had missed the complexity of the subject.

A month before, I heard a similar remark by a client who was seeing me for depression. He had just read *Reason in Pastoral Counseling* and also doubted that I knew what I was talking about because it sounded oversimplified. In time he learned that what I had to say about controlling depression really was quite simple, but that using that knowledge was another story entirely. The same is true for this material on anger. When I suggest that you always make yourself angry by thinking you have to have your way and that that is all there is to this matter of anger, I also confess it sounds over-simplified. Yet that is basically all that anger is.

Don't be misled into thinking that the task of controlling yourself will ever be easy just because it is simple. You will doubtless at times find yourself forgetting everything you learned and still explode or rationalize yourself into a state of fury. This will happen many times, I can assure you. Many of you will even wonder if you will ever get on top of this problem. To help you avoid being too harsh with yourself, however, let me define for you what progress means. If you change the intensity, frequency, and duration of your angry episodes, you're making progress. That means that if you get angry once a month rather than once a week (frequency), you've made improvement. If you only raise your voice when you usually struck with your fist (intensity), that's improvement. And finally, if your anger, even if it is severe, only lasts an hour now but once lasted all day (duration), that's improvement. And if you keep on making improvement like that, however slight, the day will come when you will look back over a period of months when you haven't had a real bad scene at all. And when you can look back over several years without seeing a really heated, angry incident, then you're qualified to write a book on the subject.